From Overwhelmed to Organised: A Time Management Blueprint For Busy Professionals

Take Control of Your Time and Your Life: The Ultimate Guide to Getting Organised and Achieving Maximum Success

Toyin Obafemi

Copyright 2023 by Toyin Obafemi

Published by Pnuxel Consulting
toyin@pnuxelconsulting.com

All rights reserved. No part of this book may be reproduced or transmitted in any form or by any means- electronic or mechanical, including photocopying, recording, or by any information storage and retrieval system without the author's written permission except for the inclusion of brief quotations in a review.

Contents

Acknowledgements 6

From Overwhelmed to Organised: A Time Management Blueprint for Busy Professionals 8

Chapter One: Maximising Your Time For Maximum Success 11

    The Benefits of Being Organised 16

Chapter Two: Identifying and Prioritising Your Goals 24

    Discover The 3 Most Important Goals In Your Life: A Quick And Easy Guide 26

    Setting Clear and Specific Goals 31

    Dream Big, Achieve More: A Step-By-Step Guide for Busy Professionals To Set Clear And Specific Goals For Professional And Personal Success 47

Chapter Three: Determining Which Tasks Are Most Important 50

    1. The Pareto Principle 51

    2. The ABCDE Technique 59

    3. Time Management Matrix 67

    Learn To Say "NO" 73

Get Things Done: A No-Nonsense Guide to Task Management 81

Chapter Four: Scheduling And Planning 84

Creating A Daily Schedule 85

Using A Planner or Calendar Effectively 99

Delegating Tasks and Seeking Help 101

Chapter Five: Managing Email And Communication 104

Setting Up an Email System That Works For You 105

Communicating Effectively and Efficiently 113

Chapter Six: Staying Focused And Avoiding Distractions 119

Identifying And Eliminating Distractions 120

Using Techniques Such as The Pomodoro Technique To Increase Focus. 138

Chapter Seven: Getting Things Done: Productivity Tips and Tricks 160

Identifying And Using the Right Tools And Resources 161

Implementing Productivity Routines and Habits 166

Chapter Eight: Managing Stress And Maintaining Work-Life Balance **177**

    Identifying And Reducing Stressors 180

    Setting Boundaries and Maintaining A Healthy Work-Life Balance.. 189

    Seeking Support from Family, Friends And Colleagues When Needed. 197

Chapter Nine: Wrapping Up And Maintaining Progress **201**

    Reviewing Progress and Adjusting As Needed .. 202

    Staying Motivated And Committed To Time Management And Organisation 206

Chapter Ten: Conclusion **209**

    Encouragement To Continue the Journey To Becoming Organised And Effective In Time Management. 210

Unlock Your Potential: Discover the Transformative Power of My Other Books **213**

The Author **215**

References..**218**

ACKNOWLEDGEMENTS

First and foremost, I want to give all glory and honour to God, the giver of time, life, and opportunity. Without Him, none of this would be possible.

My deepest gratitude goes to my beautiful wife, Temitope, for her unwavering support and encouragement throughout this journey. Her belief in me and this project has been a constant source of motivation. Her love and patience have been invaluable; I could not have done this without her.

I would also like to thank our precious children, Oreofe and Inioluwa, for being a source of inspiration. Their joy and curiosity remind me of the importance of living in the present and making the most of every moment.

I am also deeply grateful to Adewobi Adebanjo for bringing my vision for the cover design to life. His creativity and attention to detail have resulted in a cover that truly captures the book's essence. I also want to thank everyone who helped choose the right cover design and contributed, especially Oyedele Bolu and Dr Adebola Olajunyi. Their insights and feedback were invaluable in developing this book's cover.

Lastly, thanks to all the busy professionals who inspired me to write this book. Your struggle with time management and desire for a more organised and balanced life has been the driving force behind this project. I hope this book will serve as a blueprint for you to transform your life and achieve the success and fulfillment you deserve. Thank you!

From Overwhelmed to Organised: A Time Management Blueprint for Busy Professionals

Are you drowning in a sea of to-do lists and deadlines? Do you feel like you're constantly running on empty, with no time for the things that matter? Are you feeling overwhelmed and drained by your busy schedule? Do you struggle to get things done and meet your professional and personal goals? **If so, *"From Overwhelmed to Organised: A Time Management Blueprint for Busy Professionals"* is the book you need.**

This comprehensive guide will teach you how to maximise your time for maximum success. We'll explore the importance of time management for busy professionals and the benefits of being organised. We'll also provide a step-by-step guide for setting clear and specific goals, so you can dream big and achieve more.

But goal setting is just the beginning. We'll also delve into the nitty-gritty of task management with tips and tricks for getting things done efficiently. In the section "Get Things Done: A No-Nonsense Guide to Task Management," you'll learn how to manage your tasks and get things done efficiently. We'll cover how to create a daily schedule, use a planner or calendar effectively, delegate tasks, and set up an email system that works for you. We'll even cover techniques for increasing focus, like the Pomodoro Technique, and strategies for eliminating distractions.

Of course, no time management plan is complete without the right tools and resources. We'll help you identify and use the best tools and resources for your needs and provide tips for implementing productivity habits and routines. We'll also discuss the importance of reviewing your progress and adjusting your plan.

But I understand that time management is more than just getting things done. It's also about managing stress and maintaining a healthy work-life balance. That's why I've included a chapter on identifying and reducing stressors and strategies for stress management, like rest, relaxation, and exercise. We'll also discuss the importance of setting boundaries and seeking support when needed.

Don't let anything hold you back any longer. Take charge of your life and start your journey from overwhelmed to organised with "**From Overwhelmed to Organised: A Time Management Blueprint for Busy Professionals.**" This comprehensive guide will help you maximise your time for maximum success, set clear and specific goals, and efficiently manage your tasks and stress. Read and start achieving your dreams! You can do it!

Chapter One

MAXIMISING YOUR TIME FOR MAXIMUM SUCCESS

Imagine you're a busy lawyer, doctor, or accountant, each with a full schedule and deadlines fast approaching. Whether you're a lawyer with a caseload and a court appearance, a doctor with a list of patients and a research project deadline, or an accountant with client tax returns to prepare and a filing deadline, and you've been working nonstop for days but feel like you need to catch up. Your offices are cluttered with papers, and you can't seem to find the documents you need. You're working late into the night, trying to catch up, but it feels like you're spinning your wheels. You're exhausted and stressed, and you're starting to doubt whether you'll be able to meet your deadlines.

This is a familiar story for many busy professionals. When we don't have a handle on our time, it can feel like we're constantly running to catch up. But with the right time management skills, we can take control of our schedules and use our time more effectively. By setting clear goals, prioritising tasks, and finding ways to streamline our work, we can increase our productivity and achieve more in less time.

Now imagine a different scenario. You're still a busy lawyer, doctor, or accountant, each with a full schedule and deadlines fast approaching. But this time, you're organised and in control. You have clear plans for tackling your tasks and delegate some of your workloads to your team members. You have systems for managing your emails and documents and set aside dedicated time for focused work. As a result, you can get more done in less time and feel less stressed and overwhelmed. You can meet your deadlines with time to spare, and you feel confident and capable about your work. This is the power of effective time management for busy professionals.

As a busy professional, you know first-hand the importance of maximising your time and using it effectively. With so many demands on your time, it can be easy to feel overwhelmed and disorganised. You will likely face a constant stream of emails, meetings, deadlines, family engagements and other demands on your time. It can be easy to feel like you're constantly playing catch-up and never quite getting ahead. But with the right time management skills, you can take control of your schedule, increase your productivity, and achieve your goals more efficiently. In this introductory chapter to this one-stop book on time management for you as a busy professional, we'll explore the importance of time management for busy professionals and how it can help you achieve maximum success in your career and personal life. This book is not particular about success in your profession alone but in your personal life too, as I have found that more than fulfilment at work is needed to give an individual a sense of real achievement.

Effective time management is crucial for busy professionals because it allows you to make the most of your limited time. By prioritising your tasks and focusing on what's most important, you can increase your productivity and get more done in less time. This can not only help you achieve your goals more quickly, but it can also reduce stress and improve your overall sense of well-being. In addition, good time management skills can help you balance the demands of your career with those of your personal life, allowing you to find harmony and fulfilment in both areas.

Effective time management is about more than just getting things done, however. It's also about finding balance and managing your stress levels. When you feel overwhelmed and disorganised, it can take a toll on your mental and physical health. By implementing strategies for stress management and finding ways to maintain a healthy work-life balance, you can improve your productivity and overall health.

We were created to be in control and, more importantly, to control our time to fulfil our vision and goals. *When you are in control of your time, then you are in control of your life.* Some people miss this point as they relate time to money which is only partially accurate. Time is more valuable than money, as time is life. Once we are not in control of our time and life, we feel overwhelmed and tend to malfunction: this can express itself in the breakdown of our physical and mental health. Some professionals deprive themselves of sound mental and physical health because they are out of control of their time. This also cost them their relationships and success in their personal lives. They sacrifice the time needed to invest in their relationships to catch up with their goals and demands at work.

They later regret their actions and try to find a way to regain the trust of their families and friends, but they may not be lucky to get it back. This further plunges them to bury their heads into work and further aggravates their situations: the more reason for this time management blueprint for busy professionals. It is my joy that you excel on both fronts: your personal and professional life.

In this book, we'll delve into the importance of time management for busy professionals and provide practical tips and strategies for getting organised, setting and achieving goals, and finding balance in your life. By following the principles outlined in this book, you can transform yourself from overwhelmed to organised and achieve maximum success in your personal and professional life.

THE BENEFITS OF BEING ORGANISED

Being organised has many benefits, both for your personal and professional life. When you're organised, you are in control and on top of things. You can get things done more efficiently and have more time to focus on the things that matter most to you. But being organised isn't just about being tidy or having a clean desk - it's about having systems and processes that help you manage your time, energy, and resources effectively.

In this section, we'll explore the various benefits of being organised. Being organised can make a big difference in your life whether you're a busy professional, a student, or a stay-at-home parent. It can help you to be more productive, reduce stress, and feel more confident and capable.

So what are the specific benefits of being organised? *For a start, it can help you save time.* When you're organised, you know where everything is and don't waste time searching for things or trying to remember where you put them. This can be especially helpful if you're working on a tight deadline or have a lot of tasks to complete. *Being organised can also help you be more efficient in your work, as you can focus on what's essential and eliminate unnecessary duties.* This can lead to increased productivity and efficiency and, ultimately, success in your career and personal life.

Among the numerous benefits of being organised, which you can likewise mention, *having more time to focus on the things that matter most to you stands out.* This is because we derive fulfilment and a sense of life when we find time to engage in what matters most. What matters most to us can also be called the *"purpose"* or the *"reason"* for our existence, so if we find time dedicated to the reason why we exist, then we will live a fulfilled and enjoyable life. Otherwise, we are in for frustration and emptiness, which can make us lose the importance of being alive. Anyone who gets to this point of utter frustration and emptiness is at risk of ending their life because they do not find any reason for being alive. *The most excellent antidote to suicide is finding a reason or purpose for being alive; that is, finding a reason why you need to wake up and work:* having a reason to see your hope come to reality.

Here are nine benefits of being organised. Of course, the list could be longer, but let's keep it to nine for brevity.

1. **Increased productivity:** When you're organised, you get to focus on what matters and that which is efficient, therefore, increasing your productivity and chance of success in your endeavours. As we will see later in this book, it is only some of what we do that gives us success. *Only about twenty per cent of our task gives us about eighty per cent of the result. So being organised allows you to focus on the job that will provide you with the most impact, therefore, increasing your productivity and success.* Moving from being overwhelmed to organised helps you get more done quickly.
2. **Reduced stress:** Being organised can help you feel more in control and reduce stress. When

you are organised, you are fearless of a plate full of deadlines and meetings. You are confident because you are so organised that you know that each task and deadline already has time allocated to it in your plan. You are also organised to the extent that you have given room to emergencies which may come up. This will reduce your stress and help you get more done quickly.

3. **Increased efficiency:** Being organised allows you to increase your efficiency. Increased efficiency is getting the most result out of a task or work input. Being organised helps you get the most impact of your energy.

4. **Improved time management:** Good organisational skills can help you manage your time more effectively. You can make the most of your limited time by setting clear goals and prioritising tasks. It would help if you never forgot that your time is limited: it is not an unlimited resource.

5. **Better decision-making:** Being organised can help you think more clearly and make better decisions. Organised people think ahead and have alternative plans for their master plan; peradventure, it fails. Therefore, they are not unnecessarily overwhelmed with a load of tasks or emergencies. They are not reactive but proactive, which helps them think clearly and make good decisions amidst chaos and confusion.

6. **Improved memory:** Being organised improves your memory because you are not overwhelmed and confused, which enhances your memory. Being organised helps you get more done in less time, which opens up time for rest which gives room to recharge and improve your memory.

7. **Increased creativity:** Being organised can help you free up mental space and allow you to think more creatively. You have room for creativity when you're not constantly catching up on

deadlines. You are well-rested and open to creativity. You also have ample time to think, which opens you to the world of imagination when you are organised.

8. **Better communication:** Good organisational skills can help you communicate more effectively. When you have all the information you need at your fingertips, you can share it more clearly and concisely. Imagine if you prepared for a presentation some hours before the presentation and when you prepared a week before the due time. You would be more organised and better communicated if you organised a week before than some hours before. This is the power of being organised. *An organised individual thinks ahead and starts preparation way back before the due date for an exhibition.* They do not need anyone to push them to begin organising before they start. On the other hand, a disorganised individual may

only remember entirely about the presentation hours before the due time.

9. **Enhanced work-life balance:** Good organisational skills can help you manage your time more effectively, allowing you to create a better balance between your work and personal life. When you have more time freed up because you have more done in no time, you have more time devoted to what matters most to you. This helps you balance your work and your personal life.

Once again, welcome to this one-stop book on time management blueprint for busy professionals. It is time to take control of your time and life and achieve the maximum success possible for you. Please put on your seat belt, and let's go for a ride from being overwhelmed to being organised.

Chapter Two

IDENTIFYING AND PRIORITISING YOUR GOALS

We have started the journey from being overwhelmed to being organised already!

Identifying and prioritising your goals is the very first step to effective time management. *The first step is not to care about your time but what you spend your time on,* so it is vital to dedicate a chapter to **"Identifying and Prioritising Your Goals"**. This step cannot be overemphasised as it is the foundation to maximising your time for maximum success in your career and personal life. When you have clear goals, it is easier to prioritise them and focus on the tasks and activities that will help you achieve them. Successful individuals have clear goals: they are known for *'clarity of purpose'*. You can make the most of your time, energy and resource by making clear goals and prioritising them as appropriate. This will save you from expending energy on irrelevant tasks and free up time for other tasks.

We do not have the whole time in the world to do everything, but we have enough to do the important tasks that will make us better and more successful. Therefore, you need to identify these high-impact goals and tasks.

It is helpful to start by considering what is most important to you before you set your goals. This could be financial freedom, excellent relationships, personal growth, or good health. Once you have identified your priorities, you can set specific, measurable, achievable, relevant, and time-bound (SMART) goals to help you achieve these goals.

DISCOVER THE 3 MOST IMPORTANT GOALS IN YOUR LIFE: A QUICK AND EASY GUIDE

This is a quick and easy guide to identifying the three most important goals in your life:

1. Get a pen and a notepad.
2. Make a list of all your life goals, at least twenty. The first three to five will be easy. The next three to five will be difficult, and the last ten will be more difficult but go on until you have listed twenty or more.
3. Next, flip to the next page of the notepad and write this *"Let's imagine that I was asked to choose just one of all the goals, while others are to be discarded, and the one I chose will be fulfilled right now, which one will have the most impact on my life? Which will give me the greatest sense of achievement, happiness, and fulfilment?"*

4. Flip back to the page where you have listed the goals. Out of the goals, which one jumps at you? Which one will answer the question above?
5. Write the answer below the question.
6. Next, cross out the goal you have chosen from your list. Now you are left with nineteen or one less than the original number on your list.
7. Again, ask yourself the question you have asked before, *"Let's imagine that I was asked to choose just one of all the goals, while others are to be discarded, and the one I chose will be fulfilled right now, which one will have the most impact on my life? Which will give me the greatest sense of achievement, happiness, and fulfilment?"*. Again, put down your answer, and cross out your chosen goal from the list.
8. Repeat the process for the last time.
9. Now, you should have your 3 most important goals in order of impact and importance.
10. These goals are meant to be prioritised, and every other task should direct you toward achieving these goals.

You can also apply the above guide to your short-term goals.

This is a simple guide to identifying your most important life goals. You can replace the goals in the guide above with tasks, and let us see which of your daily, weekly, or monthly tasks should take the most of your attention and energy. This is a tip on how you can prioritise your task. We will look into this more closely shortly.

Prioritising your goals will help you determine which ones are most important and which should be given the most attention for maximum success for your energy and time. One way to prioritise your goals and tasks is to use the Pareto Method, which involves prioritising tasks based on their importance and impact. Another option is to use the ABCDE Technique, which involves assigning a letter to each goal based on its priority, while the third option is the Time Management Matrix, which involves placing your goals and tasks in quadrants depending on their importance and urgency. Using these techniques, you can be sure that you are focusing your time and energy on the goals that will impact your life and bring success: this is a sure way to predict your future *because the best way to predict your future is to plan and create it.* We will look closely into these subjects shortly.

For example, consider the story of Maria, a busy professional who struggled with feeling overwhelmed and unfulfilled in her career. She knew she wanted to better her life but needed to figure out where to start. She needed a change, but this would only occur when she changed. To achieve a different result than she has experienced, she must alter her mindset and approach toward her life and goals. Just as the quote attributed to Albert Einstein, **"Insanity is doing the same thing over and over and expecting different results"**. After some reflection, Maria realised that her top priorities were personal growth, financial stability, and work-life balance. With these priorities in mind, she set SMART goals, including completing a certification program and reading one hour every morning before preparing for work, saving money for a down payment on a house, and establishing a regular exercise routine.

Maria assigned each goal a letter based on its priority using the ABCDE technique. She placed the certification programme, reading one hour each morning and saving for a down payment in the "A" category, as these were the most important goals to her. She placed the exercise goal in the "B" category, as it was important but not as pressing as the other goals. By prioritising her goals this way, Maria could focus her time and energy on the tasks that would help her make the most progress toward her top priorities. As a result, she felt more in control of her time and fulfilled in her career. Good story! Is that? This is the way to approach your goals and tasks.

You should pick up your pen and try the exercise above, just like Maria did before we go into the nitty-gritty of the techniques. You will free yourself from unnecessary worry and duties as you focus on what matters most and which will give you more results and fulfilment in life.

SETTING CLEAR AND SPECIFIC GOALS

Setting clear and specific goals is an essential part of effective time management. Knowing what to focus on and how to prioritise your tasks can only be easy with clear goals. If your goals lack clarity, you may feel overwhelmed and unsure of what to do next. This characteristic may currently define you, but you are on a journey to becoming organised.

You have a road map to success when you have clear and specific goals. You know what you want, what you need to do, and when to do it, which can help you stay focused and make the most of your time. This section will explore the importance of setting clear and specific goals and provide practical tips and strategies for setting and achieving them.

So what makes a goal clear and specific? A clear goal is easy to understand and visualise. It should be specific enough that you know exactly what to do to achieve it. For example, a clear goal might be, *"I will lose 10 pounds in the next three months by exercising for 30 minutes a day and eating a healthy diet."* This goal is clear because it's specific and actionable. On the other hand, a vague goal like *"I want to get in shape"* is not specific and may be difficult to achieve. Setting clear and specific goals can increase your chances of success.

Some statistics put the average success rate at eight per cent, which shows that most goals are not achieved. This is because people do not set goals in the first place but wishes, and when they do, the goals lack clarity and specificity. To make it worse, the average number of times they tried to achieve their goals is not enough. What is the average number that comes to your mind? One, two, ten, or more? While teaching a group of people, I asked this question, and I got several varied answers that differed from what I had in mind.

To achieve success, you must try hitting your goals more than once. Successful individuals are known to have failed one or more times in their lifetime but what made them stand out are two; first, they acted on their goals, for if they hadn't tried, they wouldn't have failed in the first place. You are better when you fail than not trying at all. Second, when they fail, they learn from it and give their goals another shot. They are persistent and courageous in going hard for their goals. As long as you continue trying to hit your goals, you will hit the mark and have a breakthrough, just as the *action potential* needed to kick start a chemical reaction as taught in Chemistry.

So most people fail to achieve their goals because they do not have clear goals in the first place, and to make it worse, the average time they try achieving their goals is less than one as they keep procrastinating on acting on their goals for one reason or another. That means they never tried, only wished, and wishes do not lead to success. Like the English proverb, *"If wishes were*

horses, beggars would ride." The worst enemy to achieving success is inaction and procrastination.

A vague goal cannot stand the test of time. The first step to achieving your goals is to set clear and specific goals. Very important!

Imagine you are a busy professional juggling multiple roles and responsibilities. With so much on your plate, it's easy to feel overwhelmed and need help setting clear and specific goals. To free yourself from being constantly overwhelmed, you sat down with a pen and paper and started brainstorming. You thought about your long-term goals and what you want to achieve in the short term. You realise that to get where you want to be, you need to set some specific and achievable goals for the short term.

So you made a list of your goals which are clear and specific, and broke them down into smaller, more manageable tasks. You set a deadline for each goal and the steps you need to take to achieve them. You also schedule dedicated blocks of time for focused and deep work, and set aside time for rest, relaxation and self-care. More importantly, you listed the goals in order of importance and then attended to each one after the other. How will you feel while working to achieve your goals here? Great, right? Yes, and yes!

The time spent planning for a task or a goal is far more critical than the time spent working on the task. This emphasises that you need to sharpen your axe before using it.

You will feel more focused and motivated when you have clear and specific goals. You will be able to get more done in less time, and you will feel less overwhelmed. You're able to balance your work and personal lives and still make progress toward your long-term goals. By setting clear and specific goals, you can stay organised and make the most of your limited time.

One helpful way to set clear and specific goals is to use the SMART criteria. SMART is an acronym for *Specific, Measurable, Achievable or Attainable, Relevant, and Time-bound.* Using this framework can help you create goals that are more likely to be achieved.

1. Specific goals are clear and well-defined. They should be specific enough that you know exactly what to do to achieve them. For example, instead of setting a vague goal like *"I want to get in shape,"* you could set a specific goal like *"I will lose 10 pounds in the next three months by exercising 30 minutes a day and eating a healthy diet."*

2. Measurable goals have clear criteria for success. Your goals should be quantifiable, so you can track your progress and measure your success. For example, a measurable goal might be *"I will increase my sales by 20% in the next quarter."* It is also essential to know that specific goals lead to measurable goals. When you have clear and specific goals, you can track your progress, which makes your goals measurable. For instance, if you aim to lose 10 pounds in the next three months by exercising 30 minutes a day and eating a healthy diet, it is easy to track whether you are on top of your game. You do not have to get to the third month before knowing if you are on track because your goal of losing 10 pounds is clear, specific, and measurable. If you are on track, you should have lost a third of your goal weight by the end of the first month and know if you are engaging in your daily routines as stated in the goal.

3. Attainable goals are realistic and achievable. Your goals should stretch you, but they should also be within reach. For example, if you have a busy schedule and limited time, setting a goal to run a marathon in the next week may be unrealistic. However, you should not hide behind the guise of "realistic and achievable goals" to prevent yourself from being creative and exploring your potential. *Some statistics show that most people achieve only ten per cent of* *their potential in their lifetime, and recently, it went down to as low as two per cent.*

You should dare to break records. But in so doing, you should be realistic and balanced within the limits of human ability. It takes courage to journey beyond your present limitations to explore your potential: what you can do that you have not done at the moment or what you can become that you have not. *Your potential is hidden behind the curtain of your ignorance and timidity.* Once you know that you are able and ready to break free of your cowardice, you will be courageous enough to step into the new "you" that has always been there but that you have not seen before.

Courage is in two forms: the courage to start the journey to achieving your goals and the courage to persevere on the journey. There is inertia to starting the journey to success and resistance or friction to achieving it when you are on the journey: this resistance is in the form of setbacks and failure. Successful individuals are courageous enough to ride on the wings of setbacks and failure: they learn and move on, while unsuccessful individuals will complain and back out.

New records are attainable, realistic, and achievable: it all depends on you. Understanding that you can only reach new heights if you are willing to be stretched is critical. Forging iron in a fire illustrates the resilience and determination often required to attain new records or reach new heights in any field. Just as iron must be subjected to intense heat and pressure to become malleable and able to be shaped into new forms, we must be willing to endure challenging circumstances and stretch beyond our current limits and comfort to achieve our goals.

Forging iron is not easy, as it requires skill and precision to get it right. The iron must be heated to just the right temperature and then beat with a hammer to shape it into the desired form. If the iron is not hot enough, it will be too brittle and break under pressure, and if it is too hot, it will become too soft and lose its structural integrity.

In the same way, attaining new records or reaching new heights in any field requires resilience and determination, which is common to successful individuals. We must be willing to put in the hard work and effort required to achieve our goals and to endure the challenges and setbacks that come along the way. ***We should not be discouraged by the so-called setbacks because when God sends you a gift, He wraps it with a problem.*** You will miss the gift and opportunity if you back out because of the transient setback. We must be willing to stretch beyond our current limits, take risks, and try new things, even when it means stepping outside our comfort zone. We should see challenges and setbacks as opportunities for our growth and self-discovery.

Just as iron is shaped and moulded through the fire, we must also be willing to be shaped and moulded by the challenges and setbacks that come our way. We can forge ourselves into stronger and more resilient individuals, capable of achieving great things and attaining new records by taking advantage of challenges and setbacks.

4. Relevant goals are important and should align with your values and long-term goals. Relevant goals are directly related to your values and long-term goals, which are meaningful and essential to you. They should be carefully chosen and thoughtfully pursued, as they will help you move closer to where you want to be. You are predicting and creating your future by making relevant goals that align with your core values and life goals.

One of the key benefits of setting relevant goals is that they provide focus and direction for your efforts and life. When you have clear, relevant goals, you can prioritise your time and resources more effectively and are less likely to get distracted by irrelevant or unimportant tasks.

It is also good to mention that not all reasonable goals are right for you: you decide on the right goals when you judge them against your core values and life goals. For instance, if your core value is to build a great relationship with your spouse and children, you will want to avoid picking up a job that will take you away from home for the most time, even if it is good and well paying. Or, if your long-term goal is to become an excellent software engineer, you will avoid picking up a certification course on basic suturing techniques, even if it is good. *You cannot be everything; you only need to choose the right thing that resonates with your long-term goals.*

Relevant goals can help you stay true to your values and long-term aspirations. By setting goals that align with your values, you can ensure that your actions and efforts are consistent with what is most important to you. This can help you feel more fulfilled and satisfied, as you can make a positive impact in areas that matter to you.

Setting and pursuing relevant goals is essential to personal and professional growth, as it helps you focus your efforts and stay true to your values and long-term aspirations.

<u>5. Time-bound goals have a specific deadline or time frame.</u> Time-bound goals have a specific deadline or time frame attached to them. This effectively creates a sense of urgency and focus, as it helps you understand when to achieve your goal. Successful individuals have a sense of urgency: they implement their ideas fast. They do not tarry long on thinking. They act and learn from the results of their actions. You will only have a sense of urgency if your goals are time bound.

One of the benefits of setting time-bound goals is that it helps you to stay motivated and on track. When you have a specific deadline, you are more likely to stay focused and dedicated to achieving the goal or task. This can help you avoid getting distracted by other tasks or commitments, as you can prioritise your efforts and allocate your time and resources more effectively since you know the deadline for each of the goals and tasks and the impact of each on your life.

For example, instead of simply setting a goal to *"improve your sales,"* you could set a goal to *"improve your sales by 20% in the next quarter."* This time-bound goal provides a clear target to work towards and helps you to create a plan of action to achieve it. You might set specific weekly or monthly targets and track your progress. This can help you stay motivated and on track, as you can see your progress toward your goal.

Using the SMART criteria can help you create clear and specific goals that are more likely to be achieved. Setting specific, measurable, attainable, relevant, and time-bound goals can increase your chances of success and help you make the most of your limited time.

For example, let's say you're a lawyer with a full caseload and a court appearance on the horizon. You might set a SMART goal like this: *"I will prepare for my court appearance by researching the case, outlining my arguments, and practising my presentation. I will complete this preparation by the end of next week."* This goal is specific (preparing for a court appearance), measurable (outlining and practising your presentation), attainable (you have enough time to prepare), relevant (it aligns with your long-term goal of being a successful lawyer), and time-bound (you have a specific deadline). This is an example of using the SMART criteria for a short-term goal as a lawyer. You get yourself organised for the job following this simple technique.

Or let's say you're a doctor with a full schedule of patients and a research project deadline. You might set a SMART goal like this: *"I will complete my research project by the end of the month by dedicating three hours per day to writing and data analysis. I will also enlist the help of a research assistant to assist with data collection."* This goal is specific (completing a research project), measurable (dedicating a specific amount of time per day and enlisting the help of a research assistant), attainable (you have enough time to complete the project if you stay focused and make use of available resources), relevant (it aligns with your long-term goal of advancing in your field), and time-bound (you have a specific deadline). This is another example of using the SMART criteria for a doctor planning to achieve a short-term goal.

By using the SMART criteria in setting your goals, you can increase your chance of success and make the most of your limited time as a busy professional. It is time to test this technique in setting specific and clear goals for your tasks or deadlines. Pick up your pen and put the method to work.

Once you are clear about your goals, it will be easy to set your daily tasks in order of priority, saving time and earning you better results.

Dream Big, Achieve More: A Step-By-Step Guide for Busy Professionals To Set Clear And Specific Goals For Professional And Personal Success.

1. What are your long-term career goals, and how do they align with your values and interests?
2. What short-term goals will help you work towards your long-term career goals? Remember to apply the SMART criteria.
3. What specific actions will you take daily or weekly to achieve each professional goal?
4. How will you track your progress toward each professional goal?
5. What resources or support will you need to achieve each professional goal, such as additional training or help from co-workers or a mentor?
6. How will achieving each professional goal benefit you or your organisation?
7. What challenges do you anticipate as you work towards each professional goal, and how will

you overcome them? This is an excellent way to be proactive and plan for setbacks and emergencies.

8. In addition to your professional goals, what are your personal goals, and how will achieving them contribute to your overall fulfilment and well-being?

9. Are you happy or motivated by the impact you think you will derive from achieving the above personal goals?

10. What specific actions will you take daily or weekly to achieve each personal goal?

11. How will you track your progress toward each personal goal?

12. What resources or support will you need to achieve each personal goal, such as a coach or a support group?

13. How will achieving each personal goal benefit you and those around you?

14. What challenges do you anticipate as you work towards each personal goal, and how will you overcome them?

15. How will you stay motivated and focused as you work towards your professional and personal goals, despite your busy schedule? This will help you avoid distractions.

16. How will you celebrate when you achieve each goal? This is important to keep you going on achieving other goals after you have achieved one.

Chapter Three

DETERMINING WHICH TASKS ARE MOST IMPORTANT

In today's fast-paced world, it's easy to feel overwhelmed by the seemingly endless demands on our time and energy. Whether you're a busy professional, a stay-at-home parent, or a student, you probably have a long list of tasks and responsibilities vying for your attention. That's why it's crucial to identify and prioritise the essential tasks on your list. By focusing on the tasks that truly matter, you'll be able to make the most of your time and achieve your goals more efficiently.

Remember that we do not have enough time to see to every task, but we have enough to care for high-priority tasks, which determine our success. Success is not in doing every task but in accomplishing the small essential tasks contributing to actualising our vision and life goals.

This section will explore strategies and techniques for determining which tasks are most important and how to prioritise them effectively. By the end of this section, you'll clearly understand how to prioritise your tasks and focus on the most important ones first. This way, you will take control of your time and life and achieve great success. Let's get started.

1. THE PARETO PRINCIPLE

One effective technique for determining which tasks are most important is to use the "80/20 rule," also known as the *Pareto Principle.* This rule states that roughly 80% of our results come from 20% of our efforts. In other words, only a tiny portion of our tasks disproportionately impact our outcomes. By identifying and focusing on these high-impact tasks, we can maximise our time and resources and achieve our goals more efficiently and quickly. As a busy professional, it's vital to identify which tasks fall into this 20% category and prioritise them.

For example, a doctor may find that 20% of their patients account for most of their time and energy. By focusing on providing high-quality care to these patients, they can make the most significant impact on their practice. Similarly, a lawyer may find that 20% of their cases require the most attention and time and have the highest potential for a positive outcome. They can maximise their time and resources by placing more importance on these cases. Take a pause and think about this. Let's assume that the doctor or lawyer focuses and spend most of their energy on duties that do not account for most of their results. What do you think will be the result? They might seem to work but not smartly.

When I was in school, the importance placed on each course for each semester was different. One may be a 4-unit course, another a 2-unit course, and yet another may be a unit course. We usually want the highest grade in the 4-unit course because that will significantly impact our Cumulative Grade Point Average (CGPA). Imagine if a student pays greater attention to a unit course and gets an 'A' in the course and then a 'D' in the 4-unit course. In contrast, another student gets a 'D' in the 1-unit course and an 'A' in the 4-unit course. Who will have a better grade at the end of the semester? This is an excellent illustration of the Pareto principle, which we should pay attention to as busy professionals concerning our goals and tasks.

You can improve your efficiency and productivity by identifying and prioritising the most important tasks. This can alleviate overwhelming feelings and allow you to make the most of your time. It's essential to regularly review and reassess which tasks fall into the

20% category, as priorities and workloads can change over time.

In addition to applying the Pareto principle to your tasks as a busy professional, it can also be helpful to consider this technique in your personal life. For example, a small percentage of your leisure activities or hobbies bring you the most joy and fulfilment. By prioritising these activities, you can make the most of your free time and improve your overall well-being.

Similarly, a small percentage of your relationships require the most attention and effort. By focusing on these relationships and maintaining strong connections with such relationships, you can improve your personal and social support.

It is crucial to balance your professional and personal commitments, and the Pareto principle can help you identify which tasks and activities are most important in each domain. This also calls for regular reassessment since our tasks and priorities can change with time.

Applying the Pareto principle can help you lead a more fulfilling and organised life as you know where your attention and time should be.

Practical ways on how to use the Pareto principle for busy professionals

There are several practical ways that busy professionals can use the Pareto principle to determine which tasks are most important and thus improve their time management skills.

One way is to create a task list and prioritise the tasks based on their impact and importance. Start by listing all the tasks you need to complete, and then identify which tasks will impact your goals and objectives the most. These tasks should be placed at the top of your list and given the highest priority. Consider assigning a deadline to each task to give you a sense of urgency, help you stay on track, and ensure that you're making progress.

Another way to use the Pareto principle is to track your time and analyse how you spend it. By keeping a log of how you spend your time, you can identify which tasks and activities take up the most time and which are less important. This can help you reduce your to-do list as you shelve the ones that take your time but are less important or do not impact your success. By doing this, you can comfortably reduce the task you have on your plate, free up time and take charge of your time and life.

You can also use the Pareto principle to delegate tasks to others. Concerning the less important tasks, consider delegating them to others with the skills and resources to complete them efficiently. This can free up more time for you to focus on the tasks that are most important and have the biggest impact on your goals.

Overall, the Pareto principle is a valuable tool for you as a busy professional to free up your time and take charge of your life. You can increase your efficiency and productivity by engaging in this principle. Give it a shot today. *If you need to act, then act now, as there is no result without action.*

In addition to applying the Pareto principle to professional tasks, it can also be helpful to consider its implications on your personal life. For example, a small percentage of your hobbies bring you the most joy and fulfilment. Focusing on these activities can help you get the most out of your free time and boost your overall well-being and health.

For example, let's say you enjoy gardening, cooking, and reading in your free time. By tracking your time and analysing how you're spending it, you may find that gardening brings you the most joy and relaxation. You can then prioritise gardening as your main hobby and allocate more time and resources to gardening. Alternatively, if reading is your most fulfilling leisure activity, you can make more time to read to ensure that you get enough of this activity. You should also check if these activities help you achieve your long-term personal goals.

Similarly, a small percentage of your relationships require the most attention and effort. By focusing on these relationships, you can improve your social support network. For example, you may have a close group of friends with whom you enjoy spending time and feel a strong connection. You can prioritise these friendships and make time for regular meetups or activities to strengthen them.

It's essential to balance your professional and personal commitments, and the Pareto principle can help you identify which tasks and activities are most important in each domain. By regularly reviewing and reassessing your priorities, you can ensure that you spend your time and energy on the things that matter most. Applying the Pareto principle can help you lead a more organised and prosperous life.

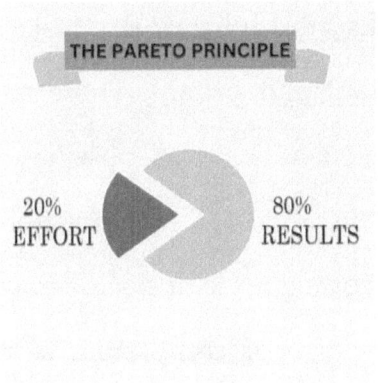

2. THE ABCDE TECHNIQUE

Another technique in deciding which tasks are more critical to increase your productivity is the "**ABCDE method**," which involves categorising tasks based on their importance and urgency.

The ABCDE method is a time management technique that can help busy professionals prioritise their tasks and make the most of their time. The method involves assigning a priority level to each task based on its importance and urgency.

Here's how the ABCDE method works:

- **'A' tasks are high-priority tasks that are both important and urgent.** These tasks should be completed as soon as possible, as they often have a deadline or a significant impact on your goals. For example, a doctor may have a high-priority task of completing a surgery report before the end of the hour, as the report is vital for the patient's care. If the 'A' task is not completed, it has significant consequences. You do not want to leave such tasks unattended. Such a task should top your list. Applying this simple strategy saves you a lot of trouble and worry.

- **'B' tasks are important but not urgent.** These tasks should be completed on time, but they may have a flexible deadline. These tasks have minor consequences if not done compared to the A tasks. The rule is you don't sit on B tasks when you have an A task on your table. For example, a lawyer may be tasked with preparing a case for trial, which is essential but not urgently needed until a few weeks. The task in this category should also top your list. Many of the tasks for personal growth fall into this category. Therefore, the more you pay attention to them, the better your life. Successful individuals spend most of their time attending to tasks in this category. Can you take a minute to list some of your tasks that fit this category? Maybe five of them.

- **'C' tasks are low-priority tasks that are less important and not urgent.** These tasks can be postponed until you have more time and energy. These tasks have no consequence if not done, unlike the A and B tasks. For example, an accountant may have the task of updating their website, which is not a priority at the moment and can be completed later.
- **'D' tasks are tasks that can be delegated to someone else.** By delegating these tasks, you can free up more time to focus on more important and urgent tasks.

- **'E' tasks are tasks that can be eliminated.** These tasks may not be necessary or may not add value to your goals and objectives. You can streamline your workflow and improve efficiency by eliminating these tasks.

Three striking features in the above technique are: *important, urgent, and consequence.* Using the ABCDE method, you need to judge your task with these three features to place it appropriately on your priority list. When the task is important and urgent, with a major consequence of you refusing to get it done, it is a high-priority task that should be in the A category. The B category task is similar to the A category as it is also a high-priority task as it is important but not urgent. Therefore if not done now, it has a minor consequence. But the B-category task can become an A-category task as it slowly becomes urgent with time, so you may want to deal with it as soon as possible before it becomes urgent. Of course, the C category task is less important and not urgent at the moment. Can you see how the three striking features help you label your task appropriately? Do not forget the task you can delegate or eliminate, the D and E tasks, respectively.

The ABCDE method can help you prioritise your tasks and make the most of your time. By identifying and focusing on the most critical tasks, you can increase your efficiency and productivity and better achieve your goals. It is also essential to regularly review your list to make necessary adjustments, as each task might change in relevance and urgency, moving up or down the ladder of priority.

In addition to using the ABCDE method to prioritise professional tasks, it can also be helpful to apply this technique to your personal life. By identifying and prioritising important and urgent tasks in your personal life, you can achieve success in your personal life.

For example, you may have a high-priority task of planning a vacation with your family, which is both important and urgent as it requires coordinating schedules and booking travel. You may also have the task of organising your home office, which is important but not urgently needed until the end of the month. By assigning a priority level to each of your tasks, you can prioritise your time and energy and ensure that you focus on the things that matter most. This way, you will not get overwhelmed with the task as you know which task can wait for later to get your attention.

The ABCDE method is valuable for managing your time and priorities in your professional and personal life. It can help you control your time and life, get organised, and achieve maximum success.

Practical ways on how to use the ABCDE technique for busy professionals

There are practical ways that busy professionals can use the ABCDE method to determine which tasks are most important, thus improving their time management skills.

One way to use the ABCDE method is to create a task list and assign a priority level to each task. Start by making a list of all the tasks you need to complete, and then consider the importance and urgency of each task. Use the definitions above to assign a priority level to each task (A, B, C, D, or E). This can help you identify which tasks should be prioritised and which can be delegated or eliminated.

Another way to use the ABCDE method is to review and reassess your task list regularly. As your priorities and workload change, adjusting each task's priority level is crucial to stay organised and focused on the most critical tasks. This will move you from overwhelmed to organised.

You can use the ABCDE method to create a daily to-do list in order of importance. By so doing, you focus on the task that most matters to you with the highest impact first and then move down the list as the day goes by. This can help you stay on track and avoid feeling overwhelmed by your workload. ***Even if you do*** *not finish the whole tasks for the day, you have cleared the ones with the most significant consequences. What a way of relieving yourself of unnecessary worry.*

In addition to using the ABCDE method to prioritise professional tasks, it can also be helpful to apply this technique to your personal life. By identifying and prioritising important and urgent tasks in your personal life, you can better manage your time and energy and lead a more rewarding and fulfilling life.

For example, let's say you have a goal of saving money for a down payment on a house, which is both important and urgent as it requires careful budgeting and saving. You can make this goal a priority in your daily to-do list and focus on tasks that will help you reach this goal, such as cutting back on unnecessary expenses and finding ways to increase your income. On the other hand, you may have a goal of learning a new language, which is essential but only urgently needed later in the year. You can assign this goal a lower priority and schedule time for language lessons or practice on a specific day or week.

The ABCDE method is a valuable tool for managing your time in your professional and personal life. You can better achieve your goals by putting most of your energy into what matters to you and delegating or eliminating others. By so doing, you will be well-spent even if you have a lot to do.

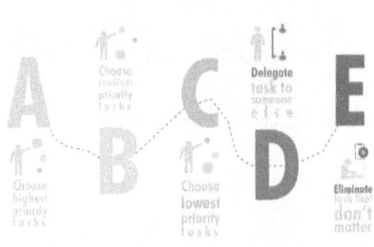

3. TIME MANAGEMENT MATRIX.

You can only be in control of your time, energy, and life and achieve great success if you know how to prioritise your tasks. Thus, here is another method found to be very useful in determining which tasks are essential and whether you should put your time and energy into them at the moment. This method is similar to the ABCDE technique. It is known as the time management matrix. You can use this matrix to prioritise your tasks, which will help you get on top of your game and be in control. Applying this method will lessen your worry as you have assigned each task to its quadrant with allocated time to attend to it.

The time management matrix is a tool that can help you determine which tasks are most important and prioritise your time and energy accordingly. The matrix is a grid that divides tasks into four quadrants based on their importance and urgency.

Here's how the time management matrix works:

- **Quadrant 1: Important and urgent tasks.** These tasks should be given the highest priority, as they often have a deadline or a significant impact on your goals. Examples of important and urgent tasks for busy professionals include completing a report for a client, attending an important meeting, or responding to a pressing email.

- **Quadrant 2: Important but not urgent tasks.** These tasks are essential, but they may have a flexible deadline. Examples of important but not urgent tasks include updating your resume, planning a long-term project, or taking a professional development course. Most personal growth activities stay in this quadrant, and successful individuals spend most of their time in it. If you want to be in control of your time and life, get organised and achieve maximum success, then spend most of your time in this quadrant.

- **Quadrant 3: Not important but urgent tasks.** These tasks are urgent but unimportant and do not help you achieve your life goals or make you successful. Examples of not-important but urgent tasks include answering non-critical emails, attending a non-essential meeting, or completing a low-priority task for a colleague.

- **Quadrant 4: Not important and not urgent tasks.** These tasks are optional and can often be delegated or eliminated. Examples of not-important and not-urgent tasks include checking social media, attending a non-essential event, watching movies or completing a low-priority personal task.

The time management matrix can help you make the most of your time. By focusing on tasks in Quadrants 1 and 2, you can increase your efficiency and productivity and better achieve your goals. This is one of the habits of wildly successful people. They have learnt how to spend more time in Quadrants 1 and 2 of the time management matrix. They spend more time on essential tasks, which impacts their lifetime goals and vision more. *You cannot spend most of your time in Quadrants 3 and 4 and expect great success.* Instead, you will find yourself using a fire-brigade approach for your important tasks because you would have wasted time on the less important tasks: this will make you feel overwhelmed by the workload, and less progress will be made.

Let's say you are a busy accountant with a full schedule at work and a busy personal life. You may have the task of planning a family holiday party, which is important and urgent as it requires coordinating schedules and booking a venue. This task would fall into Quadrant 1 of the time management matrix and should be given the highest priority.

You may also have the task of creating a budget for the upcoming year, which is essential but only urgently needed at the end of the month. This task would fall into Quadrant 2 of the time management matrix and should be given a high priority but may not need to be completed as urgently as tasks in Quadrant 1. Also, you may need to improve your knowledge in your career field: this task is necessary but not urgent. This task will fall into Quadrant 2 of the time management matrix. Though it is not urgent, it should be prioritised because it determines your growth and development and takes you a step towards your life goals.

In addition, you may have the task of attending a non-essential event, which is optional but is urgent as it is scheduled for today. This task would fall into Quadrant 3 of the time management matrix and may not need to be given as high of a priority as tasks in Quadrants 1 and 2.

Finally, you may want to watch a movie or check your social media dashboards, which are unimportant and not urgent. These tasks would fall into Quadrant 4 of the time management matrix. You should not spend time here because it does not add to your success; instead, it retards you from achieving your potential and success.

Using the time management matrix to prioritise your tasks, you can better manage your time and energy and ensure that you focus on the most important things that bring you the most benefits.

Learn To Say "NO"

Everyone, rich or poor, short or tall, male or female, black or white, has a daily twenty-four-hour allocation. We are equal regarding this allocation. No one has more or fewer hours per day, except if the individual is no longer alive. As long as you are alive, you have the same number of hours per day as everyone else to do as you wish. *Your success is determined by how well you manage the time allocated to you. Successful individuals have mastered how they invest their time, thus, their lives.* You are a product of how you have spent your time until now. Everyone should manage their time effectively and, more importantly, busy professionals.

This leads us to the lesson in this section: "Learning to Say No." Learning to say "no" is essential for managing your time effectively and achieving great success. I found it difficult to say "no" when asked to take on a task until I realised that when I say "no" to one task, I am saying "yes" to another. It is common for people who do not manage their time effectively to turn to others for help in managing their crises. While it can be tempting to take on such tasks, I have found that it is often more beneficial to decline and say "no" in these situations. Do not be afraid or feel guilty about turning down such requests. I was in the same situation until I understood that I could become unnecessarily overwhelmed with tasks I could not handle if I didn't decline them.

It can be easy to feel overwhelmed by the number of requests and obligations that come your way if you are not wise enough to refuse what you cannot handle. Like the Bible story of the ten virgins, the five foolish virgins did not plan adequately and needed the wise ones to aid them with oil. The wise virgins politely declined. They would find themselves in crises and fail together if they had not. Do you get that? Can you see that it is wise not to clog yourself with non-important and often urgent tasks from people around you?

Saying "no" doesn't have to mean being rude or uncooperative. It simply means setting boundaries and prioritising your own goals and needs. It can be helpful to consider whether a request aligns with your values and goals before accepting it. If it doesn't, it might be best to politely decline and focus on the tasks and obligations that are of high priority and impact to you.

It can be difficult to say "no," especially if you are used to taking on a lot of responsibilities. But it is important to remember that it is okay to prioritise your own needs and goals. By learning to say "no" when appropriate, you can avoid overcommitting yourself and ensure that you have the time and energy to focus on the most important tasks.

Imagine that you are a project manager at a company, and you are constantly being asked to take on additional projects, though you already have a full workload. If you don't learn to say "no" to some of these requests, you might find yourself overwhelmed and unable to complete your work to the best of your ability. By setting boundaries and prioritising your goals, you can avoid overcommitting yourself and ensure you have the time and energy to focus on the most critical tasks.

Also, imagine you are a busy parent being asked to volunteer at your child's school or participate in various community organisations. While participation in your community is good, setting boundaries and prioritising your goals are more important. By learning to say "no" to some requests, you can ensure that you have the time and energy to focus on your responsibilities as a parent and achieve your own goals. You can accept such responsibility when you are sure you have created a block of time to function adequately in such a role.

This does not apply to tasks given to you by others alone; it also includes tasks on your to-do list that do not add value to you. For instance, when you say "no" to seeing a movie, you are saying "yes" to a far more important task that will add value to you and help you achieve success. Unimportant tasks should be eliminated, as we have seen previously.

Learning to say "no" to an unimportant task will save you from unnecessary headaches and help you stay organised.

Practical ways on how to use the time management matrix for busy professionals

One effective way to utilise the time management matrix is to list your tasks and assign a quadrant to each one based on its importance and urgency. Start by compiling all the tasks that need to be completed, then consider how pressing and significant each task is. Using the above definitions, assign a quadrant to each task (Quadrant 1, Quadrant 2, Quadrant 3, or Quadrant 4). This helps you identify which tasks should be prioritised and which can be delegated or eliminated.

Another helpful approach is to review and reassess your task list regularly. This is essential to identify when each of your tasks shifts in importance and urgency. This keeps you organised over time.

To further improve your time management skill, consider creating a daily to-do list using the time management matrix. Create the list in order of importance and urgency.

Let's say you are a busy computer software engineer with a full schedule at work and a busy personal life. You may have the task of planning a surprise birthday party for your spouse in a couple of days, which is important and urgent as it requires making arrangements. This task would fall into Quadrant 1 of the time management matrix and should be given the highest priority.

You may also have the task of organising your home, which is important but only urgently needed at the end of the month. This task would fall into Quadrant 2 of the time management matrix and should be given a high priority but may not need to be completed as urgently as the tasks in Quadrant 1.

In addition, you may have the task of attending a weekly professional course, which is essential but not urgent as it is scheduled at the same time every week. This task would fall into the Quadrant 2 of the time management matrix and should be given a high priority but may not need to be completed as urgently as tasks in Quadrant 1.

Finally, you may have the task of seeing a football game that is unimportant and not urgent. This task would fall into Quadrant 4 of the time management matrix and may not need to be given as high of a priority as tasks in the other quadrants.

Using the time management matrix to prioritise your tasks, you can better manage your time and energy and ensure that you're focusing on the most important things and bring you the most reward, joy and fulfilment. Here are a few additional tips on how to use the time management matrix in your personal life:

- **Set aside dedicated time for each quadrant:** Consider setting aside specific blocks of time in your schedule to focus on tasks in each quadrant. For example, set aside the first hour of your day for Quadrant 1 tasks, the second hour for Quadrant 2 tasks, and so on. This can help you stay organised and focused on the most important tasks.
- **Use the 80/20 rule:** The 80/20 rule, also known as the Pareto Principle, states that 80% of your results come from 20% of your efforts. Consider applying this rule to your time management matrix by focusing on the tasks in Quadrants 1 and 2 that will significantly impact your goals.
- **Delegate or eliminate tasks in Quadrants 3 and 4:** To free up more time for the most important tasks, consider delegating or eliminating tasks in Quadrants 3 and 4. This can

help you reduce your workload and improve your effectiveness.

Overall, the time management matrix is a powerful tool to manage your time and energy more effectively and move you from overwhelmed to organised.

GET THINGS DONE: A NO-NONSENSE GUIDE TO TASK MANAGEMENT

The Pareto Method:

Step 1: Identify all of the tasks that you need to complete.

Step 2: Prioritise the tasks based on their importance and impact using the 80/20 rule.

Step 3: Determine the percentage of time you will spend on each task.

Step 4: Identify the tasks that have the most significant impact. These are the tasks that should be given the highest priority.

The ABCDE Technique:

Step 1: Identify all of the tasks that you need to complete.

Step 2: Prioritise the tasks based on their importance and impact.

Step 3: Assign each task a letter based on its priority:

- 'A' tasks are the most important and should be completed first.
- 'B' tasks are important but not as urgent as A tasks.
- 'C' tasks are less important and can be completed later.
- 'D' tasks can be delegated to someone else.
- 'E' tasks can be eliminated if possible.

Time Management Matrix:

Step 1: Identify all of the tasks that you need to complete.

Step 2: Draw a matrix with two axes: "urgency" and "importance."

Step 3: Place each task in the appropriate quadrant of the matrix based on its urgency and importance

- Quadrant 1: Tasks that are both urgent and important should be prioritised.
- Quadrant 2: Important but not urgent tasks should be prioritised.
- Quadrant 3: Urgent but unimportant tasks should be delegated or eliminated.
- Quadrant 4: Tasks that are neither urgent nor important should be eliminated.

By following these steps, you can determine which tasks are most important and prioritise them accordingly to ensure that you are using your time effectively. This is a no-nonsense guide to managing your time. I particularly like the time management matrix.

Chapter Four

SCHEDULING AND PLANNING

Hey there! Thanks for going this far with me in this book. Undoubtedly, you have gotten value for your time reading this far. Well, that is only a part of it, as I have more to share to help you manage your time effectively and achieve great success. The last chapter was a foundation for getting you from overwhelmed to organised. In this chapter on scheduling and planning, we'll go a little deeper and explore different strategies and techniques for organising your time, like making to-do lists and using time-blocking and calendar management tools.

Afterwards, we'll discuss staying flexible, adapting to changing circumstances, and overcoming common scheduling challenges like procrastination and time-wasting habits. By the end of this chapter, you'll have a good understanding of how to effectively schedule and plan your time to be as productive as possible and reach your goals, building on the foundation of setting priorities we covered in the last chapter.

CREATING A DAILY SCHEDULE

Like most busy professionals, you probably feel like there needs to be more time in the day to get everything done. I once had a conversation with a colleague. We both had a lot to do, and while walking the walkway, I said, "I feel like there should be an increase in the 24 hours available per day. It seems the number of hours isn't enough for me". It was as if he had been waiting for me to raise this point. He agreed quickly and reaffirmed that he likewise thought that way. "Can we get time to buy?" we joked. We also discussed the number of hours we dedicated to sleep, and it sometimes feels like we should find a way to stay awake and yet be well nourished. You must have felt this way before. That's where creating a daily schedule comes in handy. You can increase your productivity, reduce stress, and accomplish more in less time by planning your time and tasks daily. In this section of this book, "From Overwhelmed to Organised: A Time Management Blueprint for Busy Professionals," we'll talk about how to create a daily schedule that works for you.

First, we'll cover identifying your priorities and allocating your time effectively. This might involve setting aside specific blocks of time for tasks, breaks, and personal activities. For example, you might schedule a block of time in the morning for working on a project, followed by a break for lunch and then a block of time in the afternoon for answering important emails or arranging a vacation for your family. It is important to build in breaks and downtime to avoid burnout. You might schedule a short break every hour to stand up, stretch, and refocus. This is important! Many miss the aspect of breaks for daily scheduling, which made scheduling their work and goals fail.

Next, we'll discuss how to stay flexible and adjust your schedule. Things don't always go as planned, so it's important to have room in your schedule to accommodate unexpected events or tasks. You might also need to shift your schedule based on your energy levels or other personal factors. Finally, we'll discuss using tools and technologies to help you plan and track your time. Whether a paper planner or a digital calendar app, having a system to manage your schedule can make a big difference in your ability to stay organised and on track. By the end of this section, you'll have the skills and knowledge you need to create a daily schedule that helps you stay organised, avoid becoming unnecessarily overwhelmed, and achieve your goals quickly.

You may refer to our last chapter on determining which tasks are most important with the most significant impact on your overall goal.

Easy-Peasy Tips for Creating A Workable And Effective Daily Schedule

Identifying your priorities and allocating time to them are vital steps in creating a daily schedule that works. Here are a few tips to help you get started:

1. **Make a list of all your tasks and obligations for the day, week, or month.** This might include projects, appointments, and personal activities.
2. **Use a priority matrix or a similar tool to classify each task as high, medium, or low priority, as we have seen in our previous chapter.** This will help you focus on the most critical tasks first and avoid getting bogged down with low-priority tasks.
3. **Consider your energy levels when allocating your time.** Some tasks require more mental or physical energy than others. Try to schedule

your most demanding tasks during your peak energy times and save less demanding tasks for times when you feel less energised. Successful people pay attention to this and engage in tasks requiring high mental energy in the early hours of the day. It would help if you refrained from checking your emails, surfing the internet or going through your social media accounts in the early hours of the day. If you allow such a habit, you are bringing a Quadrant 4 task to the top of your schedule, which should not be. If you are fond of doing this, you must replace the habit with a better one. I did not say you should stop the habit but replace the habit because, in the real sense, habits aren't stopped but replaced. So *if you want to stop a habit, find one to replace it.* A chapter is dedicated to avoiding such distractions later in this book.

Ideas are best generated in the early hours of the day; hence you do not want to use such hours on unimportant tasks that do not have any value to your life goals and vision.

4. **Build in breaks and downtime to avoid burnout.** It is essential to take regular breaks to *rest, recharge, and refocus your attention.* I call this *the 3 R's*. You might schedule a break every hour or so, or set aside specific time for breaks.

5. **Use tools and technologies to help you plan and track your time.** This is important to keep you on track.

6. **Be flexible.** Things may come up that you did not capture in your plan. Give room for flexibility and plan around tasks taken off your list or those that surface along the way.

Following these tips will go a long way toward helping you stay on top of your game, increase your productivity, and ultimately earn you great success.

Here's an example of how a banker with professional and personal goals can use the above tips to create a daily and weekly schedule:

1. Make a list of all tasks and obligations. The banker might have several professional tasks to complete, such as preparing reports, analysing financial data, and meeting with clients. They might also have personal tasks and obligations, such as exercising, grocery shopping, and spending time with their family.
2. Use a priority matrix to classify tasks as high, medium, or low priority. The banker might prioritise their professional tasks as a high priority. In contrast, personal tasks and obligations might be classified as medium or low priority for the working days of the week.
3. Consider energy levels when allocating time. The banker might schedule their most demanding professional tasks for the morning when they have the most energy and save less demanding tasks for the afternoon. Personal tasks and obligations are scheduled for the evening when the banker's energy levels are lower.

4. Build in breaks and downtime. The banker might schedule a break every hour to stand up, stretch, and refocus their attention. They might also set aside specific blocks of time for breaks and personal activities, such as exercising or spending time with family.

5. Use tools and technologies to help plan and track time. The banker might use a digital calendar app to schedule and track their tasks and appointments.

6. Be flexible. Give room for emergencies.

Based on these tips, the banker's daily schedule might look like this:

- Before 8 am: Meditation, prayer and confession to stay positive for the day. It is good to start your day by confessing your written goals (it is an excellent step to staying organised for the day). Also, it is good to feed your mind with positive stuff (for me, I read my Bible as I have found it to be a great book full of principles, and I also listen to valuable teachings).

Again, it is great to interact warmly with your loved ones in the morning. This sets the day for each family member before they go out. Discuss and eat from the same plate if possible or at the same table: it keeps them motivated and positive with good self-esteem.

Successful people are early risers. Rise early and outline your goals for the day. Someone said it is better to outline your goals for the day the night before.

- 8:00am-12:00pm: Professional tasks (high priority): the professional tasks can accommodate the list in this category in order of priority with short breaks in between.
- 12:00pm-1:00pm: Lunch and break
- 1:00pm-4:00pm: Professional tasks (medium priority): the professional tasks can accommodate the list in this category in order of priority

- 4:00pm-6:00pm: Exercise/Meditation/Music
- 6:00pm-8:00pm: Personal tasks and obligations (medium priority): the personal tasks can accommodate the list in this category in order of priority
- 8:00pm-9:00pm: Wind down and relaxation

NB: this is not a fixed schedule. It is a simple guide; you can twerk to soothe your needs.

On the weekends, the banker might prioritise personal goals and time with their family. Their schedule might look something like this:

- Before 8am: confession, meditation, reflection, prayers, reading, exercise etc.
- 8:00am-12:00pm: Personal tasks and activities (high priority): the personal tasks can accommodate the list in this category in order of priority.
- 12:00pm-1:00pm: Lunch and break
- 1:00pm-4:00pm: Family time and activities (high priority)

- 4:00pm-6:00pm: Exercise/Music
- 6:00pm-8:00pm: Personal tasks and obligations (medium priority): the personal tasks can accommodate the list in this category in order of priority
- 8:00pm-9:00pm: Wind down and relaxation

In addition to focusing on personal goals and family time on the weekends, the banker might also make a point to schedule vacations and other personal activities as high priorities throughout the year. By intentionally creating time and planning for vacations and other personal goals, the banker can ensure that they have a well-rounded schedule that allows them to achieve their professional and personal goals.

That's not all about scheduling your tasks. Flexibility is also crucial. This helps you avoid unnecessary worry and anxiety when something you did not plan for happens. Staying flexible and being able to adjust your schedule as needed is an essential aspect of time management, especially for busy professionals who are often faced with unexpected events and changes. Here are a few tips to help you stay flexible and adjust your schedule as needed:

1. **Build in buffer time.** Set aside blocks of time in your schedule for unexpected tasks or events that might come up. This will allow you to accommodate last-minute requests or changes without feeling overwhelmed or rushed.
2. **Use a calendar app or planner to track your schedule.** This will allow you to easily move tasks or appointments around as needed, whether you need to reschedule a meeting or push back a deadline.
3. **Prioritise your tasks and be willing to let go of low-priority items.** If you have too much on your plate, consider dropping or delegating low-priority tasks among the tasks to make room for more important tasks or unexpected events.

4. **Be open to changing your schedule.** Sometimes, things don't go as planned, and that's fine. Do not be hard on yourself. Be willing to adjust your schedule as needed to accommodate changing circumstances or priorities.

Following these tips, you can stay flexible and adjust your schedule as needed. For example, if a client needs to reschedule a meeting, you can use your calendar app to move the meeting to a new time and slot in other tasks. Or, if you have a last-minute deadline, you can prioritise that task and adjust your schedule accordingly. You can ensure a well-balanced and effective schedule by remaining flexible and willing to adapt to changing circumstances.

Using tools and technologies to help you plan and track your time can be a powerful time management strategy, especially for busy professionals who need to juggle multiple tasks and obligations. Here are a few tools and technologies to help you stay organised and on track:

1. **Calendar apps.** Calendar apps such as Google Calendar https://calendar.google.com/calendar or Outlook https://www.microsoft.com/en-us/outlook-com/ can help you schedule and track your tasks and appointments. You can use these apps to set reminders, create recurring events, and share your schedule with others.

2. **Task management apps.** Task management apps such as Trello https://trello.com/ or Asana https://asana.com/ can help you create to-do lists, assign team members tasks, and track progress. These apps can benefit busy professionals who need to collaborate with others on projects.

3. **Time tracking apps.** Time-tracking apps such as Toggl https://toggl.com/ or Harvest https://www.getharvest.com/ can help track your time on different tasks and activities. This

can help identify time-wasting habits or areas where you might be able to streamline your workflow.

4. **Productivity apps.** Productivity apps such as Freedom https://freedom.to/ or Forest https://www.forestapp.cc/ can help you stay focused and avoid distractions by blocking access to certain websites or apps during specific times.

Using these tools and technologies, you can plan and track your time more effectively, stay organised, and stay on track with your tasks and goals. You do not have to learn how to use all the tools. Check them out and stick with the one that resonates with you.

USING A PLANNER OR CALENDAR EFFECTIVELY

Are you feeling overwhelmed and disorganised with your daily tasks and appointments? A planner or calendar can be your secret weapon for staying on top of your schedule and achieving your goals. Here's how to use a planner or calendar effectively:

1. **Find the right fit.** Do you prefer a digital calendar app you can access from your phone or computer or a paper planner that you can carry everywhere? Choose a tool that works for your needs and preferences, and you'll be more likely to use it consistently.
2. **Plan ahead.** Take a few minutes each day or week to schedule your tasks and appointments in your planner or calendar. This includes work projects, meetings, and personal activities. By mapping out your schedule, you'll have a clear picture of what needs to be done and when.
3. **Set reminders and alerts.** Don't let essential tasks or deadlines slip through the cracks. Use your planner or calendar to set reminders and alerts for key events, and you'll be less likely to miss out on essential tasks and opportunities.

4. **Stay flexible.** Life is unpredictable, and things sometimes go differently than planned. Be open to making changes to your schedule as needed, and review your planner or calendar regularly to ensure you're staying on track.

Using a planner or calendar effectively gives you a roadmap for success and can help you confidently tackle your tasks and appointments. Imagine being able to walk into a meeting knowing exactly what needs to be done or having a clear plan for your personal goals. With some planning and organisation, you feel more in control of your schedule.

DELEGATING TASKS AND SEEKING HELP

If you are a busy computer engineer and mom, for instance, it's important to recognise when you need help or when you can delegate tasks to others to manage your time effectively. Here are a few tips for delegating tasks and seeking help using examples relevant to your situation:

1. **Identify the tasks that can be delegated.** Not all tasks are created equal, and some tasks might be more suited for others to handle. For example, you might delegate grocery shopping or meal preparation to your spouse or a family member, freeing up time for you to focus on your work as a computer engineer.
2. **Consider the skills and expertise of others.** When delegating tasks, consider the skills and expertise of the people you assign tasks to. If someone has the necessary skills and experience to complete a task, it might be more efficient than doing it yourself. For example, if you have a colleague skilled in a particular programming language, consider delegating a task that requires that expertise to them.
3. **Communicate clearly and set expectations.** When delegating tasks, be clear about your expectations and provide any necessary resources or support. This will help ensure that tasks are completed effectively and efficiently.

For example, if you delegate a task to a team member at work, ensure to explain the goals of the task, the deadline, and any resources or support they will need to complete it.

4. **Seek help when needed.** It's okay to ask for help when you need it. Whether you need assistance with a specific task or just need someone to bounce ideas off, don't be afraid to seek help from others. For example, suppose you feel overwhelmed with your work and family responsibilities. In that case, you might seek help from a babysitter or a family member to give you a break and allow you to focus on your work.

By delegating tasks and seeking help when needed, you can save yourself a lot of trouble and anxiety; you can avoid being overwhelmed and get yourself organised and productive.

Chapter Five

MANAGING EMAIL AND COMMUNICATION

Welcome to the chapter on managing email and communication! As you know, effective time management is crucial for busy professionals who want to achieve their goals and maximise their success. In the previous chapters, we covered the importance of setting clear goals and creating a plan for achieving them, as well as strategies for scheduling and prioritising your tasks. In this chapter, we'll delve into another essential aspect of time management: managing your email and communication. As you've likely experienced, the constant influx of emails, messages, and other forms of communication can be overwhelming and distract you from your most important tasks. However, you can make the most of your time by learning how to manage your inbox, set boundaries, and use communication tools effectively. So, let's start turning the chaos of email and communication into a well-organised system!

SETTING UP AN EMAIL SYSTEM THAT WORKS FOR YOU

Are you tired of feeling overwhelmed by your inbox? It's a common problem for busy professionals, who often receive dozens or even hundreds of emails daily. The constant influx of messages can be overwhelming and make it challenging to stay organised and on top of your work. That's why it's crucial to set up an email system that works for you. This section will cover key strategies for managing your inbox and controlling it. You'll learn how to set up filters, create folders and labels, and use other tools to help you stay organised.

We'll also discuss the importance of setting boundaries and managing your email time effectively to get your work done without getting bogged down by endless messages. By the end of this section, you'll have a clear plan for managing your email and keeping your inbox under control, no matter how busy you are. So, let's get started!

There are key strategies to manage your inbox and keep it under control, even if you're extremely busy. Here are a few to consider:

1. **Set up folders and labels:** One of the most effective ways to organise your inbox is to create folders and labels for different types of emails. This will give you quick access to important emails and also save you time looking for such important emails, therefore, giving you more time to attend to other things that matter. For example, you might have a folder for important client emails, a folder for internal communication at work, and a folder for

newsletters and other low-priority messages. This can help you quickly and easily locate the emails that are most important to you. I will provide a step-by-step guide on how to do this with Gmail shortly. I have got you covered.

2. **Use filters:** Filters allow you to automatically route certain types of emails to specific folders based on your defined criteria. For example, you might set up a filter to send all emails from a specific sender to a particular folder or send emails with certain keywords in the subject line to a specific folder. This will ensure that important emails don't get lost in the shuffle. I will also share a step-by-step guide to do this with you shortly.

3. **Unsubscribe from unnecessary emails:** If you're bombarded with newsletters and other emails you don't need, it's time to start unsubscribing. Look for the "unsubscribe" link at the bottom of the emails you receive, and use it to stop the flow of unnecessary messages. This

can help reduce the number of daily emails you have to deal with.

4. **Use email management tools:** There are a variety of tools available that can help you manage your email and keep your inbox under control. For example, you might use a tool that allows you to schedule emails to be sent later or one that allows you to sleep emails until you're ready to deal with them. These tools can help you avoid distractions while you are working on your most important tasks for the day. I will provide you with links to some of the tools shortly.

By implementing these strategies, you can take control of your inbox. Try these tips and see how they can help you stay organised and on top of your email.

A Step-By-Step Guide on How to Set Up Folders And Labels On Gmail

In Gmail, a folder is also known as a label. When you create a folder in Gmail, it is called a label and is displayed in the left-hand sidebar of your Gmail account. Labels function the same way as folders, allowing you to organise your emails and keep your inbox from being clustered. You can create separate labels for different types of emails.

Here is a step-by-step guide on how to set up folders and labels in Gmail:

1. Open Gmail in your web browser.
2. Click on the "More" button in the left-hand sidebar.
3. Scroll down and click on "Create new label".
4. Type in the name for your new label and click "Create".
5. Repeat this process to create additional labels as needed.

To use your labels, simply select an email and click on the label icon (it looks like a small folder). You can then choose which label to apply to the email. You can also use the "Move to" button to move an email to a specific label.

A Step-By-Step Guide on How to Use Filters on Gmail

Here is a step-by-step guide on how to use filters on Gmail:

1. Open Gmail in your web browser.
2. Click on the "Settings" gear icon in the top-right corner of the screen.
3. Select "See all settings" from the drop-down menu.
4. Click on the "Filters and blocked addresses" tab.
5. Click on the "Create a new filter" button.
6. In the "From" field, enter the email address or domain of the sender you want to filter. You can also enter keywords or criteria in the other fields to refine your filter further.
7. Click on the "Create filter" button.
8. In the next screen, choose what you want to do with the emails that match your filter criteria.

For example, send them to a specific folder or label or automatically mark them as read.

9. Click the "Create filter" button to save your filter.

Some Examples of Email Management Tools.

Some examples of email management tools that you can use include Boomerang (https://www.boomeranggmail.com/), SaneBox (https://www.sanebox.com/), and Spark (https://sparkmailapp.com/). These tools offer a range of features, such as scheduling emails to be sent later, snoozing emails until you're ready to deal with them, and automatically sorting your emails into different folders or categories. These tools can be accessed through the provided links. Check them out and choose the one that resonates with you.

Here's a quick question: Do you know why your computer was cold when it checked its email?

Take a guess!

(pause)

Okay, ready for the answer?

The computer was cold because it left its **Windows** open!

I hope that joke gave you a bit of a laugh and helped to lighten the mood. Now that you have a solid foundation for managing your email and controlling your inbox, it's time to move on to the next section: communicating effectively and efficiently. In this section, we'll cover strategies for using email and other forms of communication to your advantage to get your work done without wasting time. We'll discuss the importance of setting clear expectations and using effective subject lines and tools like video conferencing to stay connected with colleagues and clients. By the end of this section, you'll have a clear plan for communicating effectively and efficiently, no matter how busy you are. So, let's get started!

COMMUNICATING EFFECTIVELY AND EFFICIENTLY

Welcome to this section on communicating effectively and efficiently! As a busy professional, you know how important it is to use your time wisely and focus on your most important tasks. However, constant emails, messages, and other forms of communication make it easy to get sidetracked. In this section, we'll cover strategies for using email and other forms of communication to your advantage to get your work done without wasting time.

The importance of setting clear expectations when communicating with colleagues and clients cannot be overemphasised. This might involve setting boundaries around your availability, using clear subject lines to help others understand the purpose of your emails, and using tools like video conferencing to stay connected with your team. We'll also cover the importance of using practical communication tools, such as project management software, to keep your projects on track and your team aligned.

Strategies For Using Email and Other Forms of Communication to Your Advantage.

If you are a busy banker, for instance, you know how important it is to use your time wisely and stay focused on your most important tasks. *One way to do this is by setting clear expectations around your availability for email and other forms of communication.* This might involve setting specific times of the day when you check and respond to emails or establishing clear guidelines for when and how you prefer to communicate. For example, let your clients know that you check your email at 10 a.m. and 3 p.m. each day or that you prefer to be contacted by phone rather than email for urgent matters. By setting these boundaries, you can avoid feeling overwhelmed by constant notifications and stay focused on your most important tasks.

For instance, if you're working on a tight deadline to secure a loan for a new client, you might let your colleagues and clients know that you'll be unavailable for certain periods. You can do this by setting an "out of office" message or by letting your team know that you'll be "heads down" on the loan application process and unable to respond to emails or messages. Using these boundaries, you can prevent constant interruption and remain focused on your highest-priority tasks.

Setting the above boundaries will save you the feeling of urgency in checking your emails or responding to anyone contacting you by mail or other means. It will also help those working with you know when to reach out to you. Any team member needing your attention after setting such boundaries must know that it is super-important to do so now.

Another important strategy is using clear and concise subject lines to help others understand the purpose of your emails. For example, if you're sending an email to a client about a loan application, you might use a subject line like "Loan application update" rather than something vague like "Important." This can assist you and your recipients in accessing important messages and adequately organising your communications.

Using tools like video conferencing can also be an effective way to stay connected with your team, especially if you're working remotely or have a dispersed team. For example, you can use video conferencing if you need to meet with a client outside of town. Video conferencing allows you to have face-to-face conversations without needing in-person meetings, which can be time-consuming and inconvenient sometimes. You can use video conferencing tools like Zoom or Skype to connect with your clients and colleagues and discuss important matters in real-time instead of exchanging emails, which might take more time. This way, you save time and get more time to invest in other things that matter to you.

Finally, consider using project management software to keep your projects on track and your team aligned. This might include tools like Asana or Trello, which allow you to create and assign tasks, set deadlines, and collaborate with your team in real-time. For example, if you're working on a project to secure a large loan for a new client, you can use project management software like Asana to track progress, assign tasks, and share documents and updates with your team. You can create a project in Asana and invite your team members, including your colleague John, for instance, to join the project. You can then create tasks for each process step, such as gathering financial documents, preparing the loan application, and presenting the proposal to the client. You can assign these tasks to yourself and John and use the software to track progress and share updates. By using these tools, you can stay organised and ensure that your team works efficiently and effectively.

Overall, by setting clear expectations, using effective subject lines, and utilising tools like video conferencing and project management software, you can use email and other forms of communication to your advantage and stay organised, even if you're extremely busy.

Chapter Six

STAYING FOCUSED AND AVOIDING DISTRACTIONS

Are you tired of feeling constantly overwhelmed and unable to focus on your work? Do you find yourself wasting valuable time on distracting websites or social media or constantly getting sidetracked by notifications on your phone? If so, you're not alone! In the previous chapters of this book, we've covered the importance of time management, how to identify and prioritise your goals, and strategies for managing your email and communication effectively. These skills are crucial for staying organised and on top of your game, but even the most organised person can still struggle with distractions. Whether it's the constant notifications from your phone, the lure of social media, or simply the temptation to procrastinate, it's easy to get sidetracked and waste valuable time.

In this chapter, we'll tackle one of productivity's biggest obstacles: distractions. We'll explore various techniques for managing your digital distractions and strategies for maintaining your motivation and focus when faced with distractions in any form. Whether you're a busy professional, a student, or a stay-at-home parent, these tips and tricks will help you stay on track and make the most of your time. So, if you're ready to take control of your distractions and boost your productivity, keep reading!

IDENTIFYING AND ELIMINATING DISTRACTIONS

The present century may be referred to as the most distracted, and it's easy to see why. With the proliferation of smartphones, social media, and other digital technologies, it's easier than ever to get sidetracked and lose focus. It's not uncommon for busy professionals to feel overwhelmed by the constant stream of notifications, messages, and emails coming at them from all sides.

One of the key steps in staying focused and avoiding distractions is identifying what is causing those distractions in the first place. This can be challenging, as distractions come in many forms and may be subtle. However, with some awareness and some self-reflection, you can start to identify the sources of your distractions and take steps to eliminate them.

For example, find that you're constantly getting pulled away from your work by notifications on your phone. You might consider turning off those notifications or setting specific times of the day to check your phone. Suppose you're struggling to focus because of the constant emails in your inbox. You might consider setting up automated responses or using your email application's "do not disturb" feature. And if you're having trouble staying motivated, it might be helpful to take a break, get some fresh air, or work on a new task.

By identifying and eliminating distractions, you can improve your focus and productivity and get more done in less time. This is especially important in the present century, where it's easy to get overwhelmed by the constant barrage of digital distractions. With a little planning and effort, you can take control of your distractions and stay focused on the tasks that matter most.

Here are some tips for identifying distractions that reduce your productivity.

1. **Start by listing all the things that distract you.** This might include notifications on your phone, emails, social media, chatty coworkers or friends, or anything else that takes your focus away from your work.

2. **Next, consider how often these distractions occur.** Are they constant interruptions, or do they only happen occasionally? Are they more likely to happen at certain times of the day? Understanding the frequency and timing of your distractions can help you identify patterns and plan accordingly.

3. **Once you have a list of your distractions, it's time to start brainstorming ways to eliminate them.** For example, if you're constantly distracted by notifications on your phone, you might consider turning off those notifications or setting specific times of the day to check the phone. If you get sidetracked by chatty coworkers, you might consider using noise-cancelling headphones or finding a quiet place to work.

4. **Consider the impact of each distraction on your productivity.** Some distractions, like a loud coworker or an emergency, might be more difficult to eliminate completely. In these cases,

it might be helpful to plan how to minimise their impact. For example, you might try wearing noise-cancelling headphones or taking a quick break to refocus when feeling overwhelmed.

5. **Finally, don't be afraid to experiment with different strategies for eliminating distractions.** What works for one person might not work for you, so be willing to try different approaches and see what works best for you. With a little bit of effort, you'll be able to identify the distractions that are holding you back and take steps to eliminate them, leaving you free to focus on the tasks that matter most.

Now that you have identified the distractions that interfere with your productivity. It is time to eliminate them. Here are some tips for doing that, thus boosting your productivity and putting yourself on the path to success.

1. Start by listing the distractions you've identified and the strategies you've come up with to eliminate them. This will help you keep track of your progress and stay motivated as you work to eliminate them.

2. Begin implementing your strategies one at a time, starting with the distractions that have the biggest impact on your productivity. For example, if you find that notifications on your phone are a constant distraction, you might start by turning off those notifications, putting on the focus mode on your phone, or setting specific times of the day to check your phone.

3. As you work to eliminate your distractions, be mindful of your habits and behaviours. Are there times of the day when you're more prone to getting sidetracked? Are there certain tasks that are particularly difficult for you to focus on? By understanding your tendencies, you can tailor your strategies to suit your needs better.

4. Don't be afraid to seek help if you're struggling to eliminate a particular distraction. This might involve seeking advice from a mentor or coach, asking a coworker for support, or even seeking the guidance of a professional therapist.

5. Finally, remember to be patient with yourself. Eliminating distractions isn't a one-time task but a continuous process of self-improvement. With time and practice, you'll better identify and eliminate distractions and focus on what matters most.

Useful Tools to Help You Eliminate Distractions.

Many tools are available to help you avoid digital distractions and stay focused on your work. Some options include

1 **Website blockers:** Tools like Freedom (https://freedom.to/) and Cold Turkey (https://getcoldturkey.com/) allow you to block access to distracting websites or apps during

specific times of the day. For example, use a website blocker to block social media during work hours or prevent yourself from getting distracted by online shopping while trying to focus on a project.

2. **Time tracking apps:** Tools like Toggl (https://toggl.com/) and RescueTime (https://www.rescuetime.com/) allow you to track how much time you're spending on different tasks and websites, giving you a better understanding of where your time is going as time is a resource that should be invested and not wasted. You can use this information to identify your most common distractions and take steps to eliminate them. What you put your time into or how you invest your time determines your success: this is the differentiating factor between successful individuals and those that are not.

3. **"Do not disturb" features:** Many apps and devices, including smartphones and computers,

have a "do not disturb" feature that allows you to silence notifications or block incoming calls and messages during specific times of the day. This can be especially helpful if you're working on a task that requires intense focus.

4 **Noise-cancelling headphones:** If you're easily distracted by noise or chatter, noise-cancelling headphones can be a lifesaver. These headphones use advanced technology to block out external noise, allowing you to focus on your work without being interrupted by your surroundings. You can check the appropriate store to get one.

5 **Focus music:** Apps like Focus@Will (https://www.focusatwill.com/) and Noisli (https://www.noisli.com/) offer a selection of background music and sounds designed to help you focus and block out distractions.

Please familiarise yourself with the tools and use them as and when due.

Apart From the Above, Here Is The Greatest Tool I Have Found In Eliminating Distractions.

In the previous sections, we've covered a range of strategies for staying focused and avoiding distractions. All of these strategies are important for staying on track and making progress towards your goals, but there's one tool that I've found particularly effective in eliminating distractions. You may be wondering what this tool is and how to engage it. I will share this all-time effective tool in this section and how to effectively engage it. Before I mention the tool, let's lay the foundation to understand the tool better. So, let's get started!

As you may know, discipline is the practice of training your mind and actions to follow a set of rules or a specific course of action. It involves developing good habits, setting boundaries, and adhering to standards or expectations. This is especially important to stay on track at work and to achieve a set goal. ***The antidote to***

distraction is discipline: being able to do what you are supposed to do at the right time and place. If you are not unnecessarily distracted, then you are disciplined. It takes discipline to stay on track, as there will always be things that will compete for your attention.

There is more to discipline than the above, as the force behind it can be within or without. This leads us to the subject called self-discipline. When the force behind keeping you on track to success is within, it is called self-discipline. Self-discipline is the ability to control your thoughts, actions, and behaviours all by yourself. It involves setting goals and working towards them without being pushed by anyone, even when you don't feel like it or when there are distractions around you. Self-discipline is often considered a key component of success and can be especially important for busy professionals who must stay focused and on track.

One striking difference between discipline and self-discipline is that discipline is often imposed from the outside, while self-discipline is self-motivated. For example, discipline might be imposed by a teacher, parent, or boss, while self-discipline comes from within.

Additionally, discipline tends to focus on following rules or standards, while self-discipline focuses more on personal growth and achievement.

Another difference between discipline and self-discipline is that discipline tends to be more reactive, while self-discipline is proactive. Discipline is often used to correct or prevent negative behaviours, while self-discipline is proactively working towards a specific goal or objective and avoiding negative behaviours that will deter the individual from achieving the goals.

Again, discipline and self-discipline can have different effects on your overall well-being. Discipline may be seen as a form of punishment or control, which can lead to feelings of resentment or frustration. Self-discipline, on the other hand, can lead to a sense of accomplishment and personal growth, helping you feel more fulfilled and satisfied with your life and work.

Thus far, we have considered various tools like web blockers, time-tracking apps and devices with "do not disturb" features that can help eliminate distractions. However, I have found that one tool stands above the rest when it comes to eliminating distractions and is thus the greatest of all: ***self-discipline fueled by a passion for a lifetime vision or goal.***

Self-discipline is the most powerful discipline on earth, and there is no greater self-discipline than one driven by a passion or inner strength to achieve a lifetime goal or vision. When you are convinced and passionate about a lifetime vision, you will be self-disciplined and able to overcome any form of distraction. This is the most incredible tool of all. Prayer and fasting can't do what this tool can. The answer to your prayers and fasting for overcoming distractions is insight and passion for a lifetime goal and vision. Without self-discipline fueled by a passion for a goal, every other tool to eliminate distractions will fail.

No motivational force can be compared to the energy or passion for achieving a lifetime goal or vision. Nothing can quench such motivation as long as the individual is convinced of it.

Conviction about a lifetime or short-term goal is more than just talking about it. It is an inner energy and belief in the vision. Anyone who gets to this point can discipline themselves to align appropriately to achieve the vision.

Passion is a strong and intense emotion or enthusiasm for something. It's a feeling that drives you to pursue your interests with energy and dedication. Passion is a powerful source of motivation, helping you stay focused and committed to your goals. The energy derived from passion can break boundaries and go through any problematic situation. A passionate man cannot be discouraged because their source of courage is within and not from their outer environment. The only thing that can stop a passionate man is discouragement from within. As long as they do not lose sight of what they have seen about themselves that others have not seen, they cannot be discouraged.

Interestingly, what is supposed to be a discouragement to them fuels them to action and gives them more energy as they see it as a motivation to their goals.

History is full of passionate men who tread the paths of difficulty and discouragement in strength and courage because they are convinced of their life vision and goals. *One thing is common to them; they are self-disciplined.* They need no one to tell them what they are supposed to do because their motivation is from within. While no one watches, they get to work and are not easily distracted.

Passion can fuel self-discipline by providing a strong sense of purpose or meaning. When you're passionate about something, you're more likely to be motivated to work towards the goals, even when it's not easy. Additionally, passion can help you stay focused and avoid getting sidetracked by distractions, as you're more likely to be engaged and invested in your work. Passionate individuals do not have the time for gossip, unnecessary chats and other distractions since their goals are usually bigger than them, and they are pressed to make every minute count to achieve the goals. They work as though the time allocated to them is not enough to achieve their goals; thus, they are buried in their work and are not easily sidetracked. So if you are distracted and have tried several strategies with no success, here is the ultimate solution: *self-discipline fuelled by a passion for a lifetime vision.* Every other thing falls in place when you get this right.

Here are a few ways in which passion can help you eliminate distractions:

1. **Passion provides motivation:** When you're passionate about your goals, you're more likely

to work towards them, even when you're busy or overwhelmed. This can help you stay focused and avoid getting sidetracked by distractions.

2. **Passion helps you stay engaged:** When you're passionate about your goals, you're more likely to be engaged and invested in your work. It is said that *'Empty Barrels Make the Most Noise.'* Passion for a lifetime goal keeps you engaged and unavailable for distractions.

3. **Passion helps you stay committed:** Passion can help you stay committed to your goals, even when there are setbacks or obstacles. By staying committed and focused on what you're passionate about, you can eliminate distractions and make progress towards your goals. Your lifetime goals allow you to direct all your efforts and short-term goals towards an ultimate one.

4. **Passion provides a sense of purpose:** When you're passionate about your goals, it gives a sense of purpose and meaning. This can help

you stay focused and motivated, even when facing challenges or distractions. This explains why some people render service without seeking payment, for instance. They are not motivated by the money rendered but by the joy and fulfilment they derive in their service: they have found meaning in their actions. *No motivation can be compared to this.*

5. **Passion helps you stay organised:** When you're passionate about your goals and vision, you're more likely to be organised and prepared. This can help you stay on top of your tasks and avoid distractedness. The thoughts of your goals take you over, makes you work and get yourself prepared and organised.

6. **Passion inspires creativity:** Passion can inspire creativity and help you develop new and innovative ideas. This can help you stay engaged and focused on your work, even when you're facing distractions. Creators are passionate. While creating, passion helps them

stay on what they have seen that others have not seen, even if things are not working as planned until they see them happen. Passion unlocks creativity!

Self-discipline fuelled by a passion for a lifetime vision is a powerful tool for eliminating distractions and staying focused on your work and goals. By finding something you're passionate about and working towards it with dedication and self-discipline, you can stay motivated and on track, no matter what challenges or distractions come your way.

USING TECHNIQUES SUCH AS THE POMODORO TECHNIQUE TO INCREASE FOCUS.

Like many busy professionals, you may find it challenging to focus on a task for long periods. Whether working on a long-term project or trying to get through your daily to-do list, staying focused can be tough when constantly interrupted or pulled in different directions. That's where the Pomodoro Technique comes in handy.

The Pomodoro Technique is a time management method developed in the 1980s by Francesco Cirillo. It involves breaking down work into short, focused bursts of time, separated by short breaks. The idea is that you can increase productivity and avoid burnout by working in short, focused bursts. The Pomodoro Technique is based on the idea that staying focused for short periods is easier than working long stretches without a break.

This section will cover the basics of the Pomodoro Technique and how to use it to increase your focus and productivity. We'll also discuss some of the benefits of using the Pomodoro Technique and how it can help you stay organised and on track. So, let's learn how to use the Pomodoro Technique to increase your focus and get more done!

The Pomodoro Technique: How A Student's Struggle Became a Global Phenomenon

The Pomodoro Technique was developed in the 1980s by Francesco Cirillo, a student at the University of

Perugia in Italy. At the time, Cirillo was struggling to manage his time effectively to complete his studies. He noticed that he was more productive when he focused on one task for a short time rather than trying to work for long stretches without a break.

Cirillo used a tomato-shaped kitchen timer to track his work, which inspired the technique's name as the Italian word for tomato is Pomodoro. The Pomodoro Technique involves working in short, focused bursts of time, followed by short breaks. The Pomodoro Technique is based on the idea that it's easier to stay focused and avoid distractions when you work in short, focused bursts rather than trying to work for long stretches without a break.

Cirillo first wrote about the Pomodoro Technique in a self-published book, "The Pomodoro Technique". Since then, the Pomodoro Technique has become a popular time management method used by individuals and organisations worldwide.

The Pomodoro Technique has also inspired some variations and adaptations, including the allowance for longer bursts of work, and another modification, which adds gaming elements to the process. Today, many tools and resources are available to help people implement the Pomodoro Technique in their daily lives, including apps, software, and physical timers. The Pomodoro Technique has helped people increase their productivity and manage their time more effectively.

Tomato-shaped kitchen timer

The Basics of The Pomodoro Technique.

As seen in the last section, the Pomodoro Technique is a simple but effective time management method that can help you stay focused and increase productivity. It involves working in short, focused bursts of time, separated by short breaks. You can avoid burnout and maintain focus for extended periods by working in short, focused bursts.

Here's how the Pomodoro Technique works:

1. Choose a task to work on.
2. Set a timer for 25 minutes (this is known as a "Pomodoro").
3. Work on the task until the timer goes off.
4. Take a short break (usually 5-10 minutes).
5. After four *Pomodoros*, take a longer break (usually 20-30 minutes).
6. Repeat the process until the task is complete.

The Technique is based on the idea that staying focused is easier when you work in short, focused bursts rather than working for long stretches without a break. Regular breaks allow your brain to rest, recharge and refocus, which can help you stay focused and avoid burnout.

It is a flexible method that can be adapted to fit your needs and schedule. You can adjust the length of the Pomodoro and breaks to suit your preferences, and you can also use the Pomodoro Technique to manage various tasks, from long-term projects to daily to-do lists. So give the Pomodoro Technique a try and see how it can help you increase your focus and productivity!

As a busy marketer and father, for instance, you may have a lot of demands on your time and energy. The Pomodoro Technique can help you stay focused and manage your time more effectively, so you can get more done and still have time for the things that matter most.

Here's how you might use the Pomodoro Technique daily:

1. Choose a task to work on. For example, let's say you need to write a marketing plan for a new campaign.
2. Set a timer for 25 minutes (a "Pomodoro"). During this time, work on the marketing plan and try to minimise distractions as much as possible.
3. Take a short break (5-10 minutes) when the timer goes off. Use this time to stretch or grab a drink of water.
4. After four pomodoros, take a longer break (20-30 minutes). You might use this time to take a walk, spend some time with your family, or catch up on a hobby.
5. Repeat the process until the task is complete. If you need to work on the marketing plan for several hours, you might take four 25-minute pomodoros followed by a more extended break, and then repeat the process until the task is done.

Using the Pomodoro Technique, you can stay focused, minimise distractions, and avoid burnout while getting things done. It's a flexible method that can be adapted to fit your needs and schedule, whether you're a busy marketer, a busy father, or just someone who wants to be more productive. So why wait? Give the Pomodoro Technique a try today and see how it can help you increase your focus and productivity!

Managing Distractions, Interruptions, and Emergencies While Using the Pomodoro Technique.

When using the Pomodoro Technique, distractions, interruptions, and emergencies can be especially disruptive. They can pull you away from your work, break your focus, and make it difficult to get back on track. So how can you respond to these types of distractions while you're in the middle of a task using the Pomodoro Technique?

One strategy is to set boundaries around your work time. For example, you might let people know you'll be unavailable for some time as you will be busy with your work and ask them to hold off on interrupting you unless it's an emergency. You might also use some of the tools used to avoid distractions which we have discussed before. You might also want to read the chapter on identifying and eliminating distractions for better understanding.

If you get interrupted, it's important to be proactive about managing the interruption. Here are a few steps you can follow:

1. **Acknowledge the interruption.** Let the person know you're aware of the interruption and that you'll get back to them as soon as possible.
2. **Assess the situation.** Is the interruption an emergency that requires immediate attention, or can it wait until your next break or the end of the Pomodoro?
3. **Act.** If the interruption is an emergency, deal with it quickly and then return to your work. If

it's not an emergency, you can schedule a time to deal with it later.

We can call this **the 3 A's approach** to minimising distractions while using the Pomodoro Technique.

Being proactive and setting boundaries around your work time can help minimise distractions and stay focused while using the Pomodoro Technique.

The "Inform, Negotiate, Call Back" Strategy: A Simple Way to Minimize Distractions While Using the Pomodoro Technique

One effective strategy for minimising distractions while using the Pomodoro Technique is the *"inform, negotiate, call back" strategy.* This approach helps you manage interruptions in a way that allows you to stay focused on your work while still being responsive to others' needs. Here's how the "inform, negotiate, call back" strategy works:

1 **Inform.** When you're interrupted, let the person know you're in the middle of a task and ask if it can wait until your next break or the end

of the Pomodoro. You might say something like, "I'm sorry, I'm in the middle of a task, and I'm trying to stay focused. Can I get back to you in 25 minutes or at the end of my Pomodoro?"

2. **Negotiate.** If the person needs your help or attention immediately, try to negotiate a solution that works for both of you. For example, you might suggest you work on the task for a few more minutes and then take a break to help the person.

3. **Call back.** If you cannot negotiate a solution, agree on a time to "call back" and deal with the issue. This might be at the end of your Pomodoro, during your next break, or at a specific time later in the day.

Using the "inform, negotiate, call back" strategy, you can minimise distractions and stay focused while using the Pomodoro Technique. It's a simple but effective way to manage interruptions and stay on track with your work. Try it out and see how it can help you increase your focus and productivity!

Let's assume you are an engineer and in the middle of a Pomodoro when a distraction arises. You can use the "inform, negotiate, call back" strategy to minimise the impact of the distraction. Here's how you might use it:

1. **Inform.** Let's say you're in the middle of a pomodoro and interrupted by a colleague who needs your help with a project. You might say something like, *"I'm sorry, I'm in the middle of a task, and I'm trying to stay focused. Can I get back to you in 25 minutes or at the end of the task?"*

2. **Negotiate.** If the colleague needs your help immediately, try to negotiate a solution that works for both of you. You might suggest you work on the task for a few more minutes and then take a break to help the colleague.

3. **Call back.** If you cannot negotiate a solution, agree on a time to "call back" and deal with the issue. This might be at the end of your Pomodoro, during your next break, or at a specific time later in the day.

It's a simple but effective way to manage interruptions and stay on track with your work, even when you're a busy professional with many demands on your time. Try it out and see!

9 Benefits of Using The Pomodoro Technique For Busy Professionals.

Using the Pomodoro Technique can have several benefits for busy professionals. Here are a few benefits of using this time management method:

1. **Increased focus and productivity:** The Pomodoro Technique can help you stay focused and get more done in less time. For example, as a busy lawyer, you might use the Technique to work on a legal brief in focused 25-minute bursts, with regular breaks in between. Working this way increases your focus and productivity and gets the brief done more quickly.
2. **Improved time management:** The Pomodoro Technique can help you manage your time more

effectively, so you can prioritise your work and avoid wasting time on tasks that aren't important. For example, as a teacher, you might use the Pomodoro Technique to plan your lesson preparation and grading, so you can focus on the most important tasks first and avoid getting bogged down in less important tasks.

3. **Reduced stress and burnout:** The Pomodoro Technique can help you reduce stress and burnout by taking regular breaks and avoiding multitasking. For example, as a busy entrepreneur, you might use the Pomodoro Technique to work on your business in focused 25-minute bursts, with regular breaks in between. You can reduce stress and improve your overall health by taking breaks and focusing on one task at a time. You can also use your breaks to do activities that help you rest, relax and recharge, such as walking. Doing this

allows you to stay energised and avoid burnout as you work.

4. **Greater work-life balance:** The Pomodoro Technique can help you make the most of your time, so you can get your work done and still have time for the things that matter most to you. For example, as a marketing professional, you might use the Pomodoro Technique to work on a marketing campaign in focused 25-minute bursts, with regular breaks in between. This can help you get the campaign done more quickly, giving you more time to spend with your family.

5. **Enhanced creativity and innovation:** Taking breaks can help stimulate your creativity and allow you to approach problems from new angles. For example, as a software developer, you might use the Pomodoro Technique to work on coding in focused 25-minute bursts, with regular breaks in between. During your breaks, you might take a walk or do some other activity

that helps you think creatively. This can help you approach coding problems from new angles and develop innovative solutions.

6. **Increased motivation:** The Pomodoro Technique can help you stay motivated by breaking down large tasks into smaller, more manageable chunks. For example, as a writer, you might use the Pomodoro Technique to work on a book in focused 25-minute bursts, with regular breaks in between. By breaking the book down into smaller chunks, you can stay motivated, consistently make progress, and prevent boredom and burnout.

7. **Improved memory and retention:** Regular breaks can help improve your memory and retention, allowing your brain to process and retain information more effectively. For example, as a student, you might use the Pomodoro Technique to study for a test in focused 25-minute bursts, with regular breaks in between. Taking breaks allows your brain to

process and retain information more effectively, which can improve your memory and retention.

8. **Enhanced problem-solving skills:** The Pomodoro Technique can help you approach problems more systematically, leading to better problem-solving skills. For example, as a project manager, you might use the Pomodoro Technique to work on a project in focused 25-minute bursts, with regular breaks in between. By breaking the project down into smaller chunks and working systematically, you can improve your problem-solving skills and get the project done more efficiently

9. **Improved teamwork:** You can improve teamwork and collaboration by setting clear boundaries and expectations around work time. For example, as a team leader, you might use the Pomodoro Technique to set clear expectations around work time and breaks. By doing this, you can create a culture of teamwork and collaboration within your team, which can

lead to better results and increased productivity.

These are just a few benefits of using this technique to improve your focus and productivity, bringing you from being overwhelmed to being organised irrespective of how busy you are.

Tools For Implementing the Pomodoro Technique: Applications and Software To Boost Your Focus And Productivity

Many different applications, software, and websites are available to help people implement the Pomodoro Technique. These tools can be handy for busy professionals who need to manage their time effectively and stay focused. Here are a few examples of tools you can use to implement the Pomodoro Technique with relevant links to them:

1. **Pomodoro Timer (website):** This simple, user-friendly website (https://pomofocus.io/) allows you to set your Pomodoro duration and break

Staying Focused and Avoiding Distractions

times, including a timer to help you keep track of your work and break periods.

2. **Focus To-Do:** This comprehensive task and time management app (available on iOS and Android) includes a built-in Pomodoro timer, as well as features like task lists, reminders, and a habit tracker. Whether on a mobile phone, a computer or a tablet, you can record tasks or start a Pomodoro anytime or anywhere using this application. https://www.focustodo.cn/

3. **Forest:** This unique app (available on iOS and Android) gamifies the Pomodoro Technique by planting virtual trees that will die if you leave the app. This can be a fun and motivating way to stay focused and avoid distractions. https://www.forestapp.cc/

4 **TomatoTimer (website):** This simple, user-friendly website (https://tomato-timer.com/) offers a customisable Pomodoro timer and a range of valuable features, including the ability to track your pomodoros and set goals.

5 **Toggl (website and mobile app):** This management tool (available on iOS and Android, as well as on the web) includes a Pomodoro timer, as well as features like project tracking, budgeting, and team collaboration. https://toggl.com/

6 **Be Focused (mobile app):** This app (available on iOS) includes a Pomodoro timer, as well as features like task lists, progress tracking, and customisable break activities.

7 **Timely (website and mobile app):** This time management tool (available on iOS and Android, as well as on the web) includes a Pomodoro timer, as well as features like project tracking, team collaboration, and automatic time tracking. https://timelyapp.com/

8. **FocusList (mobile app):** This app (available on iOS) combines the Pomodoro Technique with the concept of "deep work" to help you increase focus and productivity. It includes features like task lists, progress tracking, and customisable break activities. https://focuslist.co/

9. **Habitica (mobile app):** This gamified task management app (available on iOS and Android) includes a Pomodoro timer, as well as features like task lists, progress tracking, and rewards for completing tasks. Habitica can help make the Pomodoro Technique more fun and engaging by turning your tasks into a game. https://habitica.com/static/home

Go through the tools and stick to the one that resonates with you.

Thus far, we have looked at practical ways to identify and eliminate distractions and stay focused. More importantly, we looked at different tools and resources to help you stay focused and eliminate distractions, thus increasing your productivity and growth. Among these tools, we looked at a vital tool necessary for you to maximise other tools. As we have seen previously, this vital tool is self-discipline fueled by a passion for a lifetime vision.

Chapter Seven

GETTING THINGS DONE: PRODUCTIVITY TIPS AND TRICKS

As a busy professional, it's essential to have strategies to help you get things done efficiently and effectively. Whether working on a major project, managing a team, or juggling multiple tasks, it's crucial to have tools and techniques to help you stay organised and focused. In this chapter, we'll explore a range of productivity tips and tricks to help you get things done and achieve your goals.

One key aspect of increasing productivity is setting clear goals and priorities. By identifying what's most important and focusing on those tasks first, you can make the most of your time and avoid wasting energy on less important tasks. You'll also want to consider how to manage your time effectively, whether that means setting aside specific times for certain tasks, using techniques like the Pomodoro Technique to increase focus, or delegating tasks to others when appropriate.

In addition to setting goals and managing your time, there are other strategies to boost your productivity. In this chapter, we will build on what we have discussed in previous chapters.

IDENTIFYING AND USING THE RIGHT TOOLS AND RESOURCES

Identifying and using the right tools and resources is one key aspect of getting things done and increasing productivity. Whether you're a teacher preparing lesson plans, a marketing professional creating social media campaigns, or an entrepreneur managing multiple businesses, having the right tools and resources can greatly improve your ability to get things done efficiently and effectively. Whether you need tools to help you manage your time, stay organised, or eliminate distractions, there are resources available that can help you succeed in your role.

Many different tools and resources are available to help you boost your productivity, and it's essential to find the ones that work best for you and your needs. Task management apps, like Trello or Asana, help some people stay organised and on track. Others may find that time-tracking tools, like Toggl or Timely, help them stay focused and manage their time effectively. Still, some others may find that productivity apps, like Forest or Freedom, help them eliminate distractions and stay focused.

So, how do you identify and use the right tools and resources to boost your productivity? Here are a few tips to consider:

1. **Identify your needs:** The first step is identifying what you need in a tool or resource. Do you need something to help you manage your time? Stay organised? Eliminate distractions? Once you have a clear idea of what you need, you can start looking for tools and resources that meet those needs.

2. **Research and compare:** Once you know what you're looking for, it's time to start researching and comparing different tools and resources. There are many options out there, so it's important to do your due diligence and find the ones that are the best fit for you. Consider factors like functionality, user reviews, cost and compatibility with your other tools and systems.

3. **Test and evaluate:** Once you've narrowed down your options, it's a good idea to test and evaluate the tools and resources you're considering. This might involve trying out a free trial or demo version or asking for

recommendations from colleagues or friends who have used the tool. You can better understand whether a tool or resource is right for you before committing to it by testing and evaluating.

4. **Keep an open mind:** Don't be afraid to try new tools and resources, even outside your comfort zone. Sometimes, tools that are a little bit different or unexpected can make the biggest difference in your productivity.

5. **Customise and optimise:** Once you've found a tool or resource that works well for you, take the time to customise and optimise it to your needs. This might involve setting up preferences, integrating with other tools and systems, or creating custom templates or workflows. You can improve your tools and resources by customising and optimising your tools and resources.

6. **Stay current:** Technology and tools are constantly evolving, so it's important to stay

current and use the most up-to-date and effective tools and resources. You may want to update the tools as and when due to enjoy new and improved features. You may also want to keep an eye on new tools, which may be better than what you are used to. Things are changing and changing fast.

7. **Don't be afraid to switch:** If a tool or resource isn't working for you, don't be afraid to switch to something else. Your needs and priorities will likely change over time, and it's important to have tools and resources that meet those needs. By being open to change and trying out new tools and resources as needed, you can ensure that you're always using the best tools and resources for your needs.

8. **Get feedback from previous users:** When considering a new tool or resource, getting feedback from people who have already used it can be helpful. This might involve reaching out to colleagues or friends who have used the tool

or reading online reviews or user forums. By getting feedback from previous users, you can better understand how the tool or resource has worked for others and whether it might be a good fit for you.

9. **Use a combination of tools:** Finally, remember that no single tool or resource will be the perfect fit for everyone. You may need to use a combination of tools and resources to meet your productivity needs. Don't be afraid to mix and match different tools and resources to find the right combination for you.

IMPLEMENTING PRODUCTIVITY ROUTINES AND HABITS

The Connection Between Routines and Habits: How To Improve Your Productivity And Well-Being

Routines are regular patterns of behaviour or activity that are followed regularly. They can involve any activity, such as work tasks, personal habits, or daily routines.

For example, a daily work routine might involve waking up at a specific time, getting dressed, having breakfast, and starting work at a specific time. A personal habit routine might involve exercising at a specific time each day or taking time to meditate or reflect each morning.

Routines can be helpful because they provide structure and predictability in our lives. Following a routine can help you better manage your time and energy and avoid feeling overwhelmed or disorganised. Routines can also help us form good habits, break bad ones, and contribute to our overall well-being and sense of accomplishment.

Habits are behaviours or actions we automatically do without consciously thinking about them. Habits are not formed by chance. They are often formed through repetition, which is where routines come into play. Habits can be positive or negative.

Positive habits are behaviours that are beneficial to our well-being and success. Examples of positive habits might include exercising regularly, eating a healthy diet, reading books or getting enough sleep. Positive habits can help us feel better, look better, be more productive and perform better in our daily lives.

Negative habits are behaviours that are harmful to our well-being and success. Examples of negative habits might include procrastination, overeating, or spending too much time on screens. Negative habits can hinder our productivity, well-being, and overall success.

Habits can be difficult to change, but it is possible to form new habits or break existing ones with effort and discipline, which boils down to forming a routine and sticking to it. The ability to stick to the routine is called discipline, and self-discipline is the most effective discipline. The energy that fuels self-discipline is from within, and the best of these energies is passion, which is formed from the conviction and desire to fulfil a lifetime vision. By establishing new routines and practices and by sticking to them through self-discipline, we can work to develop positive habits and break negative ones.

Habits are not broken in the real sense but replaced. If you want to break a habit, then replace it with another, and the new one will displace the old. Getting accustomed to the new habit helps you lose touch with the previous one.

Routines and habits are related in that routines can help us develop habits. As we have seen before, a routine is a regular pattern of behaviour or activity followed regularly. On the other hand, habits are behaviours or actions that we do automatically, without consciously thinking about them.

Establishing a routine can help us create structure and predictability in our lives, which can, in turn, assist us in forming good habits and breaking bad ones. For example, if we establish a routine of exercising every day at a specific time, we can develop the habit of exercising regularly. Similarly, if we establish a routine of going to bed at a specific time each night, we can develop the habit of getting enough sleep.

On the other hand, habits can also influence our routines. For example, if we have the habit of procrastinating, we might need help establishing a routine of getting work done on time. In this case, it might be necessary to work on breaking the habit of procrastination to establish a more productive routine.

Overall, routines and habits are interconnected in that routines can help us develop habits, and habits can influence our routines. By establishing good routines and habits, we can increase our productivity and well-being and achieve our goals more effectively.

It is essential to know that we form habits, and later, the habits form us. We are the outcome of our routines and habits. By paying attention to our routines and habits, we can predict whether or not we will succeed.

One of the quotes about habits "we are what we repeatedly do. Excellence, then, is not an act but a habit." This quote highlights the idea that our habits shape who we are and how we live. We can become more productive, healthy, and successful by developing good habits. On the other hand, if we develop negative habits, they can hold us back and prevent us from achieving our goals.

In many cases, we form habits without even realising them. For example, we might start running every morning because we want to get in shape, and then gradually, running becomes a habit. Similarly, we might start checking our phones every time we have a spare moment, and then gradually, phone checking becomes a habit.

Habits can be a powerful force in our lives. By being aware of our habits and working to develop good ones, we can positively shape ourselves and our lives. Therefore, it's essential to be mindful of the habits we form, as they can ultimately shape us and our lives in ways that we might not even realise.

The Importance of Consistency In Achieving Success: How Routines And Habits Can Help.

Consistency is a crucial factor in achieving success, whether in your personal or professional life, and it is closely related to habits and routines. It involves maintaining a regular pattern of behaviour or activity over time. It can help you create a sense of stability and predictability to support your goals and priorities.

One way to be consistent is by establishing habits and routines that support your goals and priorities. For example, if your goal is to be more productive at work, establish a routine of starting work at the same time each day, taking regular breaks, and setting aside time for focused work without distractions. By establishing these habits and routines, you can create a sense of consistency in your work, which can help you stay on track and achieve your goals more effectively.

Consistency can also be important in following through on commitments and meeting deadlines. Being consistent in your work and personal life can build trust and credibility with others and demonstrate that you are reliable. This can be especially important in a professional setting, where your reputation and relationships with colleagues and clients can be crucial to your success.

In the business world, for instance, consistency is often seen as a key indicator of reliability and dependability. Being consistent in your work and personal life can build trust and credibility with others and demonstrate that you follow through on commitments and meet deadlines.

Get Things Done: A Practical Guide to Improving Your Consistency, Thus Your Productivity And Success.

Being consistent can be challenging, especially if you are a busy professional with a lot of demands on your time and energy. However, there are a few strategies that you can use to help you be more consistent and achieve your goals.

1. **Identify your goals and priorities:** Knowing what you want to achieve will help you create a roadmap for success and focus your efforts on the most important tasks.
2. **Create a schedule and routines:** Establishing habits and routines that support your goals and priorities can create a sense of consistency and structure in your work and personal life.
3. **Use productivity tools and resources:** These tools and resources can help you stay organised, track your progress, and manage your time and energy more effectively, as we have seen

previously. Try to check them out and stick to the one that best resonates with you.

4. **Stay focused and avoid distractions:** Distractions can be a major hindrance to consistency, so it's crucial to identify and eliminate sources of distraction and maintain focus on your tasks and goals. We dedicated a chapter to identifying and eliminating distractions. You should check that out. This is important to achieve consistency and then success.

5. **Take breaks and recharge:** Consistency doesn't mean working nonstop! Taking breaks to rest, relax, and recharge is essential to avoid burnout. This is one of the significant benefits of the Pomodoro Technique.

6. **Celebrate your achievements:** You can stay motivated to continue working towards your goals by acknowledging and celebrating your successes.

7. **Be flexible and adaptable:** Life can be unpredictable, so it's essential to adjust your habits and routines in response to changes in your work or personal life.

Following the above guide can increase your consistency and help you achieve your goals as a busy professional. Remember, consistency is an important factor in success because it can help you build trust and credibility with others, manage your time and energy more effectively, and stay focused and on track to achieve your goals.

Chapter Eight

MANAGING STRESS AND MAINTAINING WORK-LIFE BALANCE

Welcome to this chapter titled "Managing Stress and Maintaining Work-Life Balance" in this one-stop book on time management for busy professionals. In the previous chapters, we've covered a range of time management techniques and strategies to help you maximise your time and get things done effectively. However, as busy professionals, it is also important to focus on managing stress and maintaining a healthy work-life balance. In this chapter, we'll delve into some tips and techniques for reducing stress, maintaining a healthy balance between work and personal life, and finding ways to rest, relax and recharge.

There was a unit I rotated through as an intern that I will always remember. The earliest closing time when I was not on call was sunset, which didn't give me an excuse not to have seen all the patients before 8 am the following morning. We had patients almost everywhere; it was crazy! And we had senior colleagues who thought we ran on something other than blood and water. I missed my wife's birthday during this rotation because I got stuck with work until midnight. You must have wondered why she got married to a medical doctor. Truly, is it a crime to marry a doctor? It was an understatement to say that I was stressed as a doctor in that unit. Sometimes we find ourselves in a horrifying position at work as busy professionals. How do we manage such stress and maintain our mental and physical health?

Whether you're a busy entrepreneur, a corporate professional, or a stay-at-home parent, you've likely experienced stress and gotten overwhelmed at some point in your life. In today's fast-paced world, it's easy to get caught up in the hustle and bustle and forget to take care of ourselves. But the truth is, it's essential to take breaks, rest, relax, and recharge to stay productive and achieve our goals. By learning how to manage stress and maintain a healthy work-life balance, we can be more focused, effective, and fulfilled in our professional and personal lives.

So, as busy professionals, in this chapter, let's start learning how to manage stress and maintain a healthy work-life balance. We'll cover various topics, from identifying stressors and developing coping strategies to setting boundaries and finding time for relaxation and fun. By the end of this chapter, you'll have a range of tools and techniques at your disposal to help you stay calm, focused, productive, and maintain a balanced work-life, no matter how busy you are.

IDENTIFYING AND REDUCING STRESSORS

In this section, we'll focus on ways to identify the sources of stress in our lives and develop strategies for reducing or eliminating them. Stress is a natural part of life and can be helpful in small doses. It can motivate us to get things done and help us perform at our best. However, when stress becomes chronic and unmanaged, it can have serious negative effects on our physical and mental health, as well as our productivity and overall well-being.

As busy professionals, it's important to be proactive in identifying and addressing life stressors. This can involve taking a closer look at our workload, relationships, and daily routines and finding ways to streamline, delegate, or eliminate tasks causing undue stress. It can also involve developing healthy coping mechanisms, such as exercise, meditation, or seeking support from loved ones.

Identifying the sources of stress in our lives is the first step in developing strategies for managing and reducing stress.

One way to identify the sources of stress is to pay attention to your body's physical and emotional responses to stress. Physical symptoms of stress can include fatigue, headaches, muscle tension, stomach problems, and changes in appetite or sleep patterns. Emotional symptoms of stress can include anxiety, irritability, difficulty concentrating, and a negative outlook. When you notice these physical and emotional symptoms, it can be helpful to take a step back and consider what might be causing them.

Another way to identify the sources of stress is to reflect on your daily activities and consider which tasks or responsibilities are causing the most stress. This can involve analysing your workload, relationships, and daily routines to identify tasks or situations causing undue stress. It can also be helpful to keep a stress diary or journal, where you can track your stress levels and the events or circumstances that might contribute to them.

Seek the help of a professional. If you're struggling to identify the sources of stress in your life or are having difficulty managing stress on your own, consider seeking the help of a mental health professional. A therapist or counsellor can help you explore the underlying causes of your stress and develop strategies for managing it.

By identifying the sources of stress in your lives, you can develop strategies for reducing or eliminating them, improving your overall well-being and productivity.

Simple Strategies for Reducing Stress and Maintaining Work-Life Balance

As a busy professional, it's important to recognise that stress is a normal and often necessary part of life. However, when stress becomes chronic or overwhelming, it can take a toll on your physical and mental health, as well as your productivity and overall well-being. That's why it's important to develop strategies for reducing or eliminating stress. Here are a few tips to get you started:

1. **Identify the sources of stress in your life:** Take some time to reflect on what is causing you stress. Is it work-related? Personal? Financial? Once you know the root causes of your stress, it will be easier to develop a plan to address them.

2. **Make time for self-care:** Taking care of your physical and emotional needs is crucial for managing stress. Make time for activities that nourish your body and mind, such as exercise, meditation, family union, or hobbies you enjoy.

3. **Set boundaries:** It's important to set clear boundaries with your work and personal life to prevent burnout. This may mean setting limits on the number of hours you work, saying no to extra projects, or setting aside dedicated time

for relaxation. When you are at work, be at work and when you are at home, be at home.

4. **Get regular physical activity:** Exercise is a great way to reduce stress and improve overall health. It can help improve mood, reduce anxiety, and increase energy levels.

5. **Take breaks and make time for leisure activities:** It's important to make time for activities that you enjoy and helps you relax. Whether reading a book, playing with your family, or going for a walk, taking breaks can help you recharge and reduce stress.

6. **Get enough sleep:** Lack of sleep can increase stress and lead to other health problems. Make sure you are getting enough rest and establish a healthy sleep routine.

7. **Eat a healthy diet:** A healthy diet can help you feel better physically and mentally. Ensure you get enough nutrients and stay hydrated to help reduce stress.

8. **Practice time management techniques:** Proper time management can help you feel more in control of your life and reduce stress. We have seen some of these techniques.
9. **Seek support:** It's important to have a supportive network of family and friends who you can turn to when you're feeling stressed. Talking to someone about your feelings can be a great way to relieve stress and get support.
10. **Avoid unhealthy coping mechanisms:** It's important to avoid unhealthy ways of coping with stress, such as turning to alcohol or drugs. These can only provide temporary relief and can lead to additional problems in the long run.
11. **Seek professional help if needed:** If you cannot manage your stress effectively, it may be helpful to seek the help of a mental health professional. They can provide you with additional support and coping strategies to help you better manage your stress.

12. **Practice relaxation techniques:** This can include deep breathing, meditation, or yoga. These techniques can help you calm your mind and body and provide a sense of relaxation.

Stress-Busting Strategies for Busy Professionals: How to Develop Healthy Coping Mechanisms and Maintain Work-Life Balance

It's easy to turn to unhealthy coping mechanisms to try and relieve stress. However, these short-term solutions can often have negative long-term consequences. Some examples of unhealthy coping mechanisms include turning to alcohol or drugs to numb stress, procrastinating and avoiding tasks, or lashing out at others. These behaviours may provide temporary relief, but they ultimately only increase stress in the long run.

On the other hand, healthy coping mechanisms can help us effectively manage stress and improve our mental and physical health. These include exercise, meditation, and talking to a trusted friend or therapist. Finding healthy ways to manage your time and prioritise tasks can also help reduce stress.

Ultimately, the key to effectively managing stress as a busy professional is to develop a toolkit of healthy coping mechanisms that work for you. Experiment with different strategies and find what works best for you. Remember, taking care of yourself is not selfish – it's essential for your overall health and well-being.

Here are some healthy coping mechanisms you can engage:

1. **Exercise regularly:** Physical activity can help reduce stress by releasing endorphins, which are chemicals that improve mood and reduce anxiety. For example, a busy lawyer might make time to run or attend a gym class on weekends to help manage stress.
2. **Get enough sleep:** Lack of sleep can increase stress and negatively impact your overall well-

being. Ensure you get enough rest by setting a consistent bedtime, creating a relaxing bedtime routine, and avoiding screens before sleep. A busy doctor might prioritise getting enough sleep by setting an alarm to remind them to start winding down and turning off their phone an hour before bed.

3. **Connect with others:** Strong social connections can provide support and reduce stress. Make time to connect with your family and friends, especially your spouse. A busy entrepreneur might make it a duty to have quality time with their family regularly. This is a proven way to ease stress.

4. **Take breaks and practice self-care:** Make sure to prioritise self-care activities, such as hobbies, relaxation techniques, or pampering yourself. A busy project manager might schedule a weekend picnic to recharge and reduce stress. All work and no play make Jack a dull boy.

5. **Set boundaries:** It's important to set boundaries with your time and energy to avoid becoming overwhelmed. This might include saying no to extra commitments or setting limits on your availability. To avoid burnout, busy social workers might set clear boundaries with their clients, such as only responding to emails during business hours.

6. **Seek professional help:** If stress is becoming overwhelming, it might be helpful to seek the support of a mental health professional.

SETTING BOUNDARIES AND MAINTAINING A HEALTHY WORK-LIFE BALANCE.

Maintaining a healthy work-life balance is essential for busy professionals to prevent burnout and improve overall well-being. Setting boundaries is an important part of achieving this balance. It's important to communicate your boundaries to your colleagues, clients, and family members and to ensure you honour your own boundaries. This can involve setting limits on your availability outside work hours, delegating tasks, and saying no to additional commitments when necessary. It's also important to make time for self-care and leisure activities, such as exercise, hobbies, and spending time with your loved ones. By setting boundaries and prioritising your well-being, you can create a better balance between your work and personal life, which can help you feel more fulfilled and successful.

Steps to Setting Boundaries and Maintaining a Healthy Work-Life Balance for Busy Professionals

1. **Identify your priorities:** Take time to consider what is most important to you personally and professionally. This could include your family, health, career, hobbies, and more. Once you know your priorities, it will be easier to set boundaries that allow you to balance your commitments. Maintaining balance is important so that you will not be successful in

your professional life, for instance, and fail in your relationship. It would be best if you won on all fronts; therefore, you must set your priorities and balance your commitment to your professional and personal life.

2. **Set clear boundaries:** Once you know your priorities, you must communicate these boundaries to others. This can involve setting limits on your availability, saying no to requests that don't align with your priorities, and setting expectations with your colleagues, friends, and family. You do not have to live to please people. Give the necessary attention to that which matters to you.

3. **Practice self-care:** Taking care of yourself is essential to maintaining a healthy work-life balance. This can include exercising, getting enough sleep, eating well, and finding time to relax and recharge. Statistics have shown that a higher percentage of doctors are stressed and prone to suicide than the general population

because they are head-deep into their work and scarcely have the time for self-care. It is not a crime to care for yourself. Be intentional about creating time to care for yourself. You should schedule time for self-care just as you do for work. Eat well, rest well, take breaks, go for vacations, take your family and friends out for dinner, etc.

4. **Manage your time effectively:** You will free up time to care for yourself and relieve yourself of stress when you manage your time effectively.

5. **Seek support:** It's okay to ask for help when needed. Whether it's asking a colleague to cover for you, hiring a babysitter, or seeking support from family and friends, there are many ways to get the help you need to maintain a healthy work-life balance. Or even seek the help of a therapist if you feel like you are drowning or as soon as you think you need one. Even if you are a medical doctor, seek the help of a therapist if you think you need it.

6. **Take breaks:** It's essential to take breaks and give yourself time to rest, relax and recharge. This could involve taking a walk outside, going for a swim, or just taking a few minutes to close your eyes and breathe. Taking breaks is not a waste of time. Instead, It is a good time to recharge to improve your efficiency.

7. **Find ways to disconnect:** It can be difficult to disconnect from work in the digital age, but it's important to make time to disconnect. Find ways to disconnect from your devices during your off hours. This is important. Do not take work home. When you are at home, be home and when you are at work, be at work. This is crucial for your mental health.

8. **Be proactive:** Don't wait until you're feeling burnt out or overwhelmed to start taking steps to maintain a healthy work-life balance. Be proactive in setting boundaries and implementing stress management strategies so

that you can avoid feeling overwhelmed in the first place.

The Benefits of Maintaining a Healthy Work-Life Balance.

In our busy world, it can be easy to get caught up in work and neglect other important aspects of our lives; therefore, setting boundaries and maintaining a healthy work-life balance is crucial for busy professionals.

Here are some benefits of setting boundaries and maintaining a healthy work-life balance:

1. **Improved physical and mental health:** By taking breaks and not overworking yourself, you can reduce stress and improve your overall physical and mental health. For example, as a lawyer, you might set boundaries by leaving work at a certain time each day to spend time with your family. Some professionals have fallen into this trap of working all day long

without paying attention to their social and mental health, and this has cost them to learn the hard way.

2. **Better relationships:** By setting boundaries and making time for non-work activities, you can improve your relationships with your family and friends. For example, as a small business owner, you might set boundaries by not working on weekends to spend quality time with your loved ones. The time you spend with your family is not a waste but an investment. Some children do not have memories of a great time with their parents because they are busy professionals. This should not be. You should balance your work and maintain an excellent relationship with your spouse, children and loved ones. When you retire from work, you will return to the family you have invested time in or one you do not have time for. You don't want to learn the hard way.

3. **Improved work performance:** When you're well-rested and not burnt out, you'll be able to perform better at work. For example, as a doctor, you might set boundaries by taking breaks and not working excessive overtime to make better decisions and provide better care for your patients.

4. **Improved productivity and focus:** By setting boundaries and maintaining a healthy work-life balance, you can avoid burnout and maintain a clear and focused mind.

5. **Enhanced well-being and happiness:** By setting boundaries and maintaining a healthy work-life balance, you can reduce stress and improve your overall well-being. For example, as a teacher, you might set boundaries by not working on the weekends, giving you time to pursue hobbies and spend quality time with your loved ones. The ultimate is to live a happy and fulfilled life. Create time to engage in what makes you happy.

6. **Increased creativity and innovation:** By setting boundaries and maintaining a healthy work-life balance, you can give your brain time to rest and recharge, leading to increased creativity and innovation. For example, as a designer, you might set boundaries by taking regular breaks throughout the day, allowing you to come back to your work with fresh ideas.

7. **Increased self-care:** You can prioritise self-care by setting boundaries and maintaining a healthy work-life balance.

These are just a few of the benefits of living a balanced work-life. Prioritise a balance work-life.

SEEKING SUPPORT FROM FAMILY, FRIENDS AND COLLEAGUES WHEN NEEDED.

It's important to remember that we don't have to go through life's challenges alone. Seeking support from family, friends, and colleagues can be invaluable for managing stress and maintaining a healthy work-life balance. Here are a few things to consider when seeking support:

1. **Identify your support network:** Think about the people in your life who are most supportive and understanding. These might be family members, friends, religious leaders, or colleagues.
2. **Communicate openly and honestly:** Be bold and share your concerns and challenges with the people in your support network. They can only help you if they know what's going on.
3. **Take advantage of resources:** Many organisations offer employee assistance programs that support stress management and work-life balance. Be bold and take advantage of these resources if they're available.
4. **Find a balance:** It's important to remember that seeking support doesn't mean leaning on others all the time. It's essential to find a balance

between seeking support and being self-sufficient.

As a busy professional, it can be easy to feel overwhelmed and alone. Remember that seeking support from others can be a vital part of managing stress and maintaining a healthy work-life balance.

In conclusion, managing stress and maintaining a healthy work-life balance is essential for busy professionals to achieve success and sound health. You can create a more balanced and fulfilling life by identifying and reducing stressors, implementing stress management strategies, setting boundaries, and seeking support when needed. Remember that asking for help and taking breaks when needed is okay. It's essential to prioritise your well-being to perform at your best and achieve your goals. By following the tips and strategies outlined in this chapter, you can manage stress and maintain a healthy work-life balance, ultimately leading to tremendous success and happiness in both your personal and professional life.

Chapter Nine

WRAPPING UP AND MAINTAINING PROGRESS

Congratulations on making it this far in this book! By now, you should have a solid foundation of skills and strategies to help you get things done efficiently and effectively and stay focused and organised in the face of busy schedules and distractions.

In this chapter, we'll wrap up our time management journey by discussing some essential tips and strategies for maintaining your progress and staying on track long-term. Whether you're just starting your time management journey or looking to fine-tune your existing systems, these tips and strategies will help you keep moving forward and continue to get things done effectively.

So let's get started! In the following pages, we'll cover a range of topics, including staying motivated and focused, maintaining your progress over time, and troubleshooting common time management challenges. Whether you're a busy professional, a student, or a parent, these strategies will help you stay organised, focused, and productive, no matter what life throws your way.

REVIEWING PROGRESS AND ADJUSTING AS NEEDED

I hope the tips and strategies I've shared throughout this book have helped you improve your time management skills. In this section, I'll discuss the importance of reviewing your progress and adjusting as needed to maintain momentum and stay on track.

As busy professionals, it's easy to get caught up in the hustle and bustle of daily tasks and lose sight of your long-term goals. That's why it's essential to regularly review your progress and make adjustments to ensure that you're staying on track and progressing towards your vision and life goals. Whether you're working on a specific project, managing a team, or juggling multiple tasks, regularly reviewing your progress can help you identify areas for improvement and make necessary adjustments to stay focused and productive. So, let's dive into the importance of reviewing progress and adjusting as needed to maintain momentum and stay on track.

It's essential to regularly review your progress and make any necessary adjustments to ensure that you are staying on track and progressing towards your goals. This is especially important for busy professionals who may have a lot on their plate and may need more time or energy to reevaluate their approach constantly. Reviewing your progress and adjusting as needed can ensure that you are making the most of your time and resources and that you can maintain momentum and stay focused on your goals. Additionally, this can help you identify any challenges or obstacles you may be facing and allow you to come up with solutions to overcome them. For example, a business owner might review their progress every quarter, identify areas where they are falling behind and adjust their strategies to get back on track. Similarly, a teacher might review their lesson plans regularly to ensure that they are meeting the needs of their students and making the most of their time in the classroom.

It's important to regularly review your progress, maintain momentum, and stay on track. Here are a few tips for how to do this:

1. **Set regular review points:** Choose a frequency that works for you, whether weekly, monthly, or quarterly. This will allow you to check your progress and see if you need to make any adjustments.

2. **Reflect on your goals:** Take a moment to think about the goals you set at the beginning of your time management journey. Are you still on track to achieve them? If not, why? Are there any roadblocks or distractions that you need to address?

3. **Consider your progress:** Have you made progress on your goals? If so, great! If not, it may be time to re-evaluate your strategy. Are there any new techniques or tools that could help you make more progress?

4. **Adjust as needed:** Make any necessary adjustments to your time management strategy based on your reflections and observations. This might involve setting new goals, delegating tasks, or finding new tools or resources to help you stay organised and focused.

5. **Celebrate your successes:** Remember to take a moment to celebrate your achievements and progress. This will help you stay motivated and keep you moving forward.

STAYING MOTIVATED AND COMMITTED TO TIME MANAGEMENT AND ORGANISATION

If you're reading this chapter, you're already committed to improving your time management skills and achieving more outstanding organisation in your personal and professional life. However, it's important to remember that staying motivated and committed to these goals can be a challenge, especially when life gets busy or you encounter setbacks or obstacles. This section will explore strategies for staying motivated and committed to your time management and organisation goals. Whether you're just starting your journey to better time management or are well on your way, these strategies can help you stay focused and motivated as you achieve greater productivity and organisation.

Here are a few strategies that can help:

1. **Set small, achievable goals:** Rather than trying to tackle everything at once, focus on small, achievable goals that you can work towards

daily or weekly. This will help you see progress and give you a sense of accomplishment. The small wins encourage and motivate you to press on.

2. **Find an accountability partner:** Having someone to hold you accountable can be a great way to stay motivated. Consider finding a colleague or friend who shares similar goals and checks in with each other regularly to discuss your progress.

3. **Celebrate your wins:** Remember to celebrate your successes along the way! Whether it's a small win like finishing a task on time or a big milestone like completing a project, it's essential to take a moment to recognise and reward yourself for your hard work.

4. **Reflect on your progress:** Take some time to reflect on your progress regularly. Think about what's working well for you, what could be improved, and what adjustments you need to

make to stay on track. This will help you stay motivated and committed to your goals.

It's important to remember that time management and organisation are continuous processes. It's about more than just getting organised once and then forgetting about it. It's about reviewing your progress regularly, adjusting as needed, and staying motivated and committed to your goals.

By implementing the strategies outlined in this chapter, you'll be able to maintain the progress you've made and continue to improve your time management and organisation skills.

Take a moment to reflect on what you've learned and how you can apply it. Then, get ready to continue your journey toward greater productivity and success. I welcome you to greatness.

Chapter Ten

CONCLUSION

This book has covered a wide range of time management strategies and techniques that can help busy professionals increase their productivity, stay focused, and achieve their goals. We have discussed the importance of setting clear and specific goals, prioritising tasks, creating a daily schedule, setting boundaries, etc. We have also explored techniques such as the Pomodoro Technique, which can help you increase your focus and avoid distractions.

One of the key points that we have emphasised throughout this book is the importance of managing stress and maintaining a healthy work-life balance. We have discussed strategies for identifying and reducing stressors, developing healthy coping mechanisms, and setting boundaries to ensure you have time for work and personal commitments.

It is important to remember that time management is a continuous process, and you may need to adjust your strategies and techniques as your needs and priorities change. By following the principles outlined in this book, you can take control of your time and achieve tremendous success in your professional and personal life.

Encouragement To Continue the Journey To Becoming Organised And Effective In Time Management.

As we come to the end of "**From Overwhelmed to organised: A Time Management Blueprint for Busy Professionals,**" it's essential to recognise that the journey to becoming organised and effective in time management is an ongoing process. *It's not something* *that you can achieve overnight or in a few days, but it's a process that takes time, effort, and commitment.* However, by following the tips and strategies outlined in this book, you can make significant progress towards becoming more organised and efficient, thus achieving great success.

Remember that being organised and effective in time management requires a combination of the right tools, habits, and strategies. It's not just about using a planner or calendar but also about setting clear goals, prioritising tasks, seeking help when needed, forming positive habits, commitment to your life goals and self-discipline fuelled by a passion for your lifetime goals and vision. It is also important to remember that the most incredible way to overcome distraction is self-discipline fuelled by a passion for a lifetime vision or goal. Also, managing stress and maintaining a healthy work-life balance is crucial for long-term success.

Don't be discouraged if you don't see immediate results. Keep working on your time management skills, and you'll see progress. And if you ever feel overwhelmed or uncertain about moving forward, just remind yourself of the benefits of being organised and the positive impact it can have on your professional and personal life. You've got this.

Unlock Your Potential: Discover the Transformative Power of My Other Books

Are you ready to take control of your life and achieve your dreams? Look no further. In addition to "From Overwhelmed to Organised: A Time Management Blueprint for Busy Professionals," I have also written other books to help guide you on your journey to success.

In **"49 Words on Marble,"** I share wisdom and inspiration through powerful affirmations and motivational quotes for men and women, young and old. Positive mindset quotes to start your day and improve your life.

"How to Live Above Circumstances" teaches you how to be in control of your life and overcome any obstacle that may come your way. **"The Beatitudes"** explores the concept of living a life of happiness, prosperity, liberty, and blessedness.

In **"Write a Book Without Breaking a Sweat,"** I share the secrets to writing a book easily, making the process less daunting and more enjoyable. **"The Role of Graphic Design and Technology in Writing"** delves into the blogging world and how to develop a successful blog harnessing technology.

Take advantage of these transformative books. Check them out today by visiting my website [https://toyinobafemi.com.ng], Amazon kindle store [https://www.amazon.com/Toyin-H.-Obafemi/e/B081TLJKH7], or searching for them in your favourite bookstores. And remember, apart from the ones mentioned here, you can get all my other books to help you achieve your goals and live the life you deserve.

THE AUTHOR

As a busy physician, author, coach, and digital solutions consultant, I understand the challenges of feeling overwhelmed and struggling to balance professional and personal goals. That's why I've written, "**From Overwhelmed to Organised: A Time Management Blueprint for Busy Professionals.**"

Through my own experiences, I've discovered the importance of time management and organisation in achieving success and living a fulfilling life. And I want to share that knowledge with you.

I've written a couple of books, all intending to help others live the life they deserve. My passion for helping others led me to set up platforms to support individuals in harnessing quality thoughts for a better life and global relevance. And I've seen firsthand the positive impact it can have on people's lives.

Although I have a background in medicine, my love for digital technology has led me to become a digital solutions consultant. And as a happily married father of two, I understand the importance of setting boundaries and maintaining a healthy work-life balance. I'm blessed to have a wonderful wife, Temitope, and two children, Oreofe and Inioluwa.

Let me guide you on your journey from overwhelmed to organised. Together, we can achieve your professional and personal goals and live the life you deserve.

I will love to hear from you. Kindly send your feedback to toyin@toyinobafemi.com.ng or leave me a review at your favourite bookstore. Thanks

Disclaimer

Please be mindful that results may vary based on individual circumstances, and the strategies and techniques outlined in this book may not be suitable for everyone.

By reading and applying the information in this book, you agree to take full responsibility for your actions and the results that may occur from implementing the strategies and techniques outlined in the book.

References

1. "Set Goals That Are Specific and Challenging". https://incafrica.com/library/marcel-schwantes-science-says-92-percent-of-people-dont-achieve-goals-heres-how-the-other-8-perce

2. "Why People Fail to Achieve Their Goals." https://www.reliableplant.com/Read/8259/fail-achieve-goals

3. "Why People Fail to Achieve Their Goals." https://www.reliableplant.com/Read/8259/fail-achieve-goals

4. "Those With Goals Are 10x More Likely to Succeed" https://www.biggerpockets.com/blog/2015-11-06-set-goals-for-2016.

5. "How Many People Reach Their Goals? Goal Statistics" https://goalscalling.com/goal-statistics/

www.ingramcontent.com/pod-product-compliance
Lightning Source LLC
Chambersburg PA
CBHW031619210526
45464CB00004B/1655